The Handbook of Costume Accessories

Diane and Giles Favell

The Handbook of
Costume Accessories

Diane and Giles Favell

THE CROWOOD PRESS

First published in 2023 by
The Crowood Press Ltd
Ramsbury, Marlborough
Wiltshire SN8 2HR

enquiries@crowood.com

www.crowood.com

British Library Cataloguing-in-Publication Data
A catalogue record for this book is available from the British Library.

ISBN 978 0 7198 4155 2

Typeset by Simon and Sons

Cover design by Maggie Mellett

Printed and bound in India by Parksons Graphics

CONTENTS

INTRODUCTION

In theatre, a costume prop is perhaps best defined as a costume accessory – such as a brooch, glasses, watch, cane, crown, hat and so on. In practice, there is sometimes a crossover of responsibility with the props department on some items – depending on how the props are used. The wardrobe department and the props department also have differing skills and equipment available, so a reciprocal cooperation can also be very beneficial.

Traditionally, costume props have been so often magically produced from carefully guarded boxes and drawers by supervisors who have collected them over many years. Many may be originals, others well-made props made for specific shows long past – but all have had their future usefulness recognized, and been placed in safe custody.

In years gone by, a morning spent at the local flea market, local junk shops and the like were good sources of period pieces. Nowadays, online auction sites seem to have taken over rather more, which involves more time for delivery and sight-unseen purchases – however, there is undoubtedly a greater range of choice available, though many 'cheap' finds may need a bit of work to produce an authentic look.

The changing world has brought other advantages to us as well. We can buy very cheap but credible jewellery components from the Far East over the internet and, very importantly, we can 'manufacture' our own pieces using affordable desk-top machines if we are so inclined. This new approach opens the door to producing our own 'designer' props in-house, or at least knowing how it can be outsourced. It should be remembered that the new skills learned are never wasted and are very satisfying to learn.

The subject being so very broad, this book can only show a very limited cross-section of examples and techniques that, of course, can be applied much more broadly with imagination. We have in some instances shown the use of (desk-top) CNC (computer numerically controlled) machines in order to demonstrate how they may be used effectively. The same props can, of course, be made using conventional tools and techniques. The idea is to fire the imagination, rather than to prescribe their use.

In this book, we have touched on some ancient skills, though we have tried to concentrate on tools and equipment that you may have (or can get quite cheaply) in the home or, if you haven't, maybe you know (or can find) someone who has. The new technologies emerging and coming into our homes through domesticating the machines are many and vast, though some basic skills in the manufacture of costume props will ensure good use of these technologies and an appreciation of authentic appearance.

We hope to bring you our combined, many years of experience in the manufacture and use of these items and, although we are merely scratching the surface of the vast subject of costume props, we hope that this may lead to an increase of interest in the skills and, hopefully, sow a seed for the furtherance of a lifetime hobby or career, such as we have had (and are having).

WORKSHOP TOOLS AND EQUIPMENT

In recent years we have become extremely fortunate that technologies that were just science fiction fifty years ago are now available to us domestically – and that benefits small workshops too.

Laser Cutting

One of the most dramatic is perhaps the laser – first successfully built in 1960, and developed over subsequent decades, lasers come in very many forms, but first came into our homes in any quantity built into CD players from the early 1980s. These were diode lasers – cheap and small – a far cry from the original ruby laser, and the gas lasers also developed.

A laser differs from other light sources in that it emits light coherently. This can be used in a number of different ways. For instance, spacial coherence can allow a laser beam to stay narrow over large distances, enabling such devices as laser pointers, or spacial coherence may allow the beam to be focused on a tight spot, allowing cutting and lithography.

1965 saw the very first laser cutter, built to drill holes in diamond dies – and heaven knows at what cost! The early 1970s enabled production of CO_2 lasers to cut such materials as textiles, as CO_2 lasers were not yet powerful enough to overcome the thermal conductivity of metals.

By the 1980s, there were more than 20,000 metal-cutting lasers in the world, and their numbers and abilities were increasing – however, they were a very significant investment, as was the control element that enabled them to be used.

Fast-forward to today – it is now possible to buy a 40W CO_2 laser from China for under £400, which may cut materials up to 5 or 6mm thick. Also available are 10W diode lasers that will cut up to 6mm.

If you wanted to buy a laser, what would you choose and why? Well, first, it depends what you want to do.

A laser can etch and it can cut, and it is one of the fastest processes of doing so. It can cut paper, card, wood, acrylic, fabric, leather, and large industrial machines can even cut metals – steel up to 15mm thick! Many other materials can be etched, including stone, glass and some metals, even with 'hobby' machines.

If you are a large concern and want to make an income from selling or making lasered products, then you will need a very capable, fast machine. In very simplistic terms, to cut through a material, you can either pump a small amount of energy into it and go slowly, or you can pump a lot of energy into it and run faster (this is very simplistic – it can be a lot more complicated than that). Therefore, if you need speed, you would need a high-powered machine, such as a large CO_2 laser, which can cost a fair bit. If you are simply doing bits and pieces for yourself, speed is not likely to be such a concern – and, therefore, either a small CO_2 or a diode laser may well be the most appropriate.

A CO_2 laser consists of a fairly large, lidded box with a work-bed at the bottom, and an enclosure at the back that houses (among other things) the static glass CO_2 tube, which generates the laser beam. The (red) light beam is then bounced sideways and forward off angled mirrors – some of which are travelling on computer-controlled linear rails – to finally bring the beam down on to the workpiece to be cut. CO_2 lasers also require cooling. The normal method is to have a water tank – or often a water chiller – under the machine, with a circulating pump, which keeps the CO_2 tube cool when it is powered up.

A diode laser (blue laser) is a much simpler affair, insofar as the laser beam is generated in a laser cartridge mounted on a computer-controlled carriage, which itself moves around in the X- and Y-planes on sets of linear rails. A minimum of 4W will be needed to be sufficient for any useful purpose.

Although lasers put out a parallel beam, it is too wide to be of use for cutting – the energy is not concentrated enough – so both types of lasers have lenses at the business end, above the workpiece, to concentrate the light beam into a tiny spot, just as a child does playing with the sun and a magnifying glass. In exactly the same way, the distance from the lens to the work to be cut is critical in order to get the spot at its hottest and most efficient. On some lasers, this Z-axis is also computer-controlled, so the lens can be lowered with the depth of cut in order to cut deeper than it would otherwise be able to do. Other lasers have the lens height set to the workpiece, and the possible cutting depth is, therefore, limited.

All lasers should have extraction. Just about everything you cut is going to generate dust or gases, and so extraction is highly recommended. The enclosed type of laser cabinet has a collar to take flexible ducting, often with a built-in fan, and may be exhausted out of the window or through a hole in an adjacent wall (sometimes via a filter). Some types of laser are 'open' (Class 4) and extraction needs to be a little more imaginative. We have a hood over our Emblaser with an in-line extraction fan, which then vents through a redundant airbrick.

They are also a fire risk, as they function by burning through materials. They should never be left alone under operation, and all sensible precautions should be taken.

Lasers are dangerous and eye protection must be worn. The frequency of the light damages the eyes and can cause blindness.

Like so many things in life, you get what you pay for. Many people have bought CO_2 lasers from China for very little money, and have found that they have needed to make alterations to get them to work or to make them safe, and that the software to control them isn't adequate – and that is a very important point. It is no good having a wonderful machine if you don't have the software to make it go.

There are companies in Europe who will supply these machines, worked over and with decent software to make them a reliable investment – but, of course, at a very significant premium. Other people do manage to find solutions very successfully, and there is a lot of information on the internet on the subject – you must really read up on the matter before making such a purchase.

Likewise there are many diode lasers to be had cheaply, and some suffer from the same lack of support; also the software side should be taken as seriously as the hardware.

There are some lasers out there that run on web-based software – meaning that your work has to go over the internet to some server somewhere for processing before it comes back to you for cutting. There may be some benefits, but there are downsides to being at the mercy of someone else's on/off switch.

When the authors looked into the subject of a suitable machine, we looked into both hardware and software before choosing to buy an Emblaser 1, which wasn't the cheapest machine available. This was a simple diode machine with a 4W business end, simple X- and Y-axes, and was supplied with Vectric Cut2DLaser software.

The machine was imported from Australia, came in kit form and took an afternoon to assemble – with absolutely no difficulty. It is also a very small machine – an A4 version was chosen, so that the whole machine fits easily on a worktop being 490 × 440mm and weighing all of 7kg – a choice that has never been regretted.

The Cut2DLaser was loaded on to a computer, instructions were followed and the provided example pattern was cut providing instant success. Weeks then followed of learning what it could really do. The manufacturers had advertised what they thought it could do, and we ran our own tests. Surprisingly, we could match them. Moreover, much finer detail than I would have thought possible was achieved with accuracy to 0.2mm.

Since Giles' 'day-job' involves the use of AutoCad and Draftsight, drawings for laser cutting were made on this software – although Cut2DLaser also has its own drawing capability, and it can import other file types and convert images into the vectors that it needs.

Generally, sheets are fixed down on to the work surface with cheap 50mm masking tape on a couple of edges, as the laser shroud is only about 2mm higher than the work, and if the sheet is slightly bowed, or lifts, the laser will catch it as it passes and move it – thus destroying the cutting job.

Fig. 1 The Emblaser 1 laser printer.

therefore, experimentation is required to ascertain the optimum cutting speed for the thickness of the material being cut. Similarly, if you do too much cutting in a small area, the acrylic can start distorting and curl up slightly towards the laser.

Given what plastics are made of, you must be aware of what you can safely cut and what you can't.

Sadly, diode lasers can't cut clear acrylic – the beam just travels straight through without touching it, due to the wavelength of the light. A CO_2 laser, however, will cut clear acrylic.

We use a laser-quality ply and MDF, which is available from a number of sources. One of the fundamental differences is the glue used, which is more sympathetic to being cut by laser.

Examples of laser cutting in this book are:

- Fourteenth-century glasses
- Leather crown

3D Printers

The other spectacular development in technology in recent years has been the emergence of affordable and practical 3D printers, now available for a few hundred pounds. Like all these CNC-based machines, a need to master some software skills is necessary in order to use them – but once you have learned the skillset for one, it is much easier to adapt to another species of machine.

For a few years the only affordable machines were FDM (fused deposition modelling) printers – filament printing – where the machine is fed by a small drum of coiled plastic filament, which is fed into a heated print-head, which is moved left and right, backwards and forwards, laying down a very fine thread of molten plastic in a precise position or line. This steadily builds up, as the build plate lowers beneath it while the object builds. In some ways this is quite crude, leaving visible 'build-lines', which are a giveaway as to its origins. It is, however, fairly strong, and reasonably quick and economical. The plastic filament is available in many colours and in many characteristics – even with

Engraving a breadboard or a piece of slate is easy, as it doesn't need fixing down. However, such jobs usually need positioning accurately, and that is achieved by taping a sheet of plain paper down first, and burning the outline of the slate (or board) on to the paper, so it is known exactly where to place it.

Wood is one of the easier materials to laser, as it doesn't do anything too unpredictable; however, other materials aren't quite so straightforward. Many plastics give off highly toxic fumes when heated, and should never get near a laser. Acrylic is one of the safe ones, but still needs extraction. As with any heat process on plastic, the laser melts as well as burns, so if you use a cutting speed that is too slow, the acrylic will re-seal itself behind the cut – which is immensely frustrating;

wood or metal as a 'filler'. It is certainly extremely useful for stage use.

More recently, resin printers have become practical in every sense – mostly in the form of DLP printers (digital light processing). These have a small resin tank at the base, underneath which is a screen (like a phone screen) that projects a picture of the cross-section of the print every 50 or 100 microns, with the build plate rising and falling above it, until the object to be printed is completed. The light of the image on the screen hardens the resin that is sitting directly above it each time it flashes on, which will be many thousand times on a large print. The resolution or detail this process gives is superb, with much smoother prints – but the whole print process can take up to two days to complete, and there isn't quite the variety of resins as there are filaments for the FDM printers.

The prints from a resin printer need to be washed off either in alcohol, such as IPA, or water for some specialist resins, and then the prints cured in light of particular frequencies.

Resin printers can give off fumes, which are best extracted to outside. Resin printers can also be temperature-sensitive – not liking lower temperatures (lower than 20℃), causing print failures.

WHAT TO PRINT?

You can draw your own designs in a 3D drawing package. The authors use DesignSpark Mechanical – a free download from RS Components – but Sketchup, Blender or countless other programs will suit. Alternatively, sites like Thingiverse.com allow the free downloading of all sorts of designs ready to print, which is extremely useful.

WHICH IS BEST?

Both types of printer have their good qualities and their weaknesses. If you are producing a larger item, or one that needs to be robust, then an FDM print is going to be most suitable; also if you need that special bracket or widget to sort that particular problem. However, if you need a very fine and beautiful piece of jewellery reproducing,

then a resin print will win hands down. To be blunt, our workshop has both – a Flashforge Finder FDM printer and a Mars 2 Pro DLP, and both get used.

Fig. 2 FDM printer – Flashforge Finder.

Fig. 3 DLP printer – Mars2 Pro DLP.

Examples printed in this book:

- Printed ring (DLP print)
- Chain of Sir Thomas More (FDM print)
- Ivory-handled cane (FDM print)

CNC Router

STEPCRAFT 420

Like so much technology, CNC tools have become affordable and useful on a small scale. One immensely useful machine is the Stepcraft 420 CNC Router.

In basic terms, this machine holds and moves a router extremely accurately, left and right, up and down, at any speed, controlled by a computer. If the machine is rigid enough and sufficiently well built, with imagination and with the help of various computer programs you can cut out very sophisticated shapes and sculpt 3D objects at a speed and accuracy that would otherwise be impractical. Materials cut can be metals through to wood and plastics. These machines range in size from about A5 paper size up to very large industrial machines.

There are many forms of CNC machines for profiling materials, including CNC mills, where the cutting head stays still and the work table moves slowly up/down, side to side and front to back underneath it. This works well for smaller metal parts, but where bigger surfaces and faster pass speeds are needed, it is simply not practical. A CNC router has a much larger static work-bed with a moving gantry spanning across it, which travels over its entire length (the 'Y'-axis). The gantry in turn carries a carriage that can travel the length of the gantry (the 'X'-axis) and, finally, this carriage carries a vertical slide (the 'Z'-axis) that carries the spindle holder – the router. By fitting stepper-motors to the gantry, the carriage and the vertical slide, you can drive and have the computer control the position of the router and its tool almost anywhere on the work-bed with tremendous precision in all three dimensions.

A good machine is well designed and well built enough that at the tool end of the router, there is absolutely no flexing, play or backlash (unwanted movement) – so the cuts will be accurate. If there is any flexing or movement, parts will come out inaccurate and the wrong size.

Workshops will use larger machines to cut plywood and timber parts for staircases and rostra, and they can be used to carve 2.5D sculpture and signage.

The authors possess a Stepcraft 420 with a KRESS 1050 FME-P spindle (router), which is a high-quality (domestic) machine with an A3-cutting capacity. These, like their larger counterparts, are designed for working in timber and plastics, although they do advertise their ability to machine aluminium. However, if a machine is well constructed, it may be even more versatile when fitted with appropriate tooling. Ours was bought primarily for profiling and machining brass and nickel-silver using carbide 'D' cutters, but will also make quick work of MDF, timber, acrylic and other materials, using conventional single- and twin-flute cutters.

Like all routers, they are noisy (not the CNC itself – just the router) and produce dust when cutting most materials. Fairly soon after acquisition an enclosure was made from 18mm MDF to keep the noise down and to control the dust. This was further lined in carpet to reduce reflected sound. Dust extraction was incorporated with a small cyclone to extract the dust and LED lights fitted. The enclosure proved remarkably effective, and the vacuum powering the extraction remains by far the noisiest element.

In order to use the machine (or any CNC machine) you need three computer programs (although some may be combined for some machines).

- Drawing program. We choose to work with DWG files and use Draftsight and AutoCad – but there are many alternatives.
- Toolpath program. We use Vectric VCarve, which also incorporates a simple drawing package as an alternative to the sophisticated drawing programs mentioned above. The primary function is

to convert the lines of the drawing into actual tool-paths for a machine to follow, creating files for -

- Post processor. We use UCCNC. This is the program that does the final translation and actually 'drives' the machine in real time.

This is certainly a learning curve, but one that pays dividends.

The bed of the Stepcraft as standard is a laminate, and is nice and flat – but not to be destroyed in service, so some spare melamine shelving was used as a 'spoil board', i.e. a work surface that gets gradually wrecked and then replaced; 18mm MDF may be used instead. This can either be held down with two clamping bars fore and aft, which prevent any movement, or fixed down with low-tack, double-sided tape (50mm). In turn, the sheet material to be cut is also taped down with double-sided tape, which thoroughly restrains any movement at all, but does allow the sheet to be carefully peeled up afterwards. If cutting material of any thickness, it can be screwed down into the spoil board – taking great care to keep the screws away from any area that will be cut.

For timbers and plastics, a single-flute cutter may be used, adjusting depth of cut and pass speed for the material.

For much work in brass, 0.8mm-diameter carbide D cutters are used to get very fine detail; they require a delicate touch and are worked extremely gently, with only 0.2mm depth and 0.25mm/second pass. At these figures they don't often break, but 2.6mm-diameter cutters can run through brass at a good depth and a greater speed with impunity.

One of the regular ways of breaking any tool is at the end of the final cut, when the finished piece breaks loose and traps the cutter and snaps it. Fortunately, the V-Carve program has a setting to add tabs – just like etches or sprues in a kit – which will hold the piece in position, keeping everything safe.

Examples of CNC routing in this book are:

- Lorgnettes
- Fourteenth-century glasses

Fig. 4 CNC router – Stepcraft 420 CNC.

Jewellery Repair

Although not conventionally within the scope of the wardrobe or costume department, it is extremely useful to have some basic jewellery-making/repair knowledge and capability in-house. Being able to make sturdy and proficient repairs to things is a great deal more satisfying than either bodging something together, or having to throw it away and replace it, as is being able to modify an existing item, or make two into one or whatever. Such knowledge is always valuable, and the developing expertise leads to better informed judgements and a greater interest in the subject.

Basic tools:

- Fine point-nosed pliers
- Fine round-nosed pliers
- Side cutters
- Small tin-snips
- Wet-and-dry 200, 400, 800, 1000 sandpaper
- Polish
- Needle files
- Jeweller's vise

Silver-solder:

- Soldering blocks
- Borax
- Easyflo silver-solder
- Silver-solder paste (Easyflo)
- Cool-paste
- Pickle
- Torch

Jewellers' supply companies, such as Cooksongold (amongst others), sell 'starter' kits for tools and for soldering, and are a very good way of starting out.

Repairs are often as simple as repairing a snapped chain, which may have a pulled link. Such issues are often rectified by using two pairs of pliers – one in each hand – and re-forming the offending link to its original form. Occasionally it is necessary to make new links or new droppers. These processes are very easy if you are equipped with suitable pliers – but not so easy without!

More complicated solutions are required when a jump-ring has snapped off a pendant or, even worse, wire glasses' frames have snapped. The only good solution with this kind of job is to use silver-solder to repair, as soft solder or glue is rarely strong enough to hold.

SILVER-SOLDERING

Silver-soldering is a process of joining metals together using a silver compound as the solder material. Also known as hard soldering, the process takes place at between 680 and 780°C (depending on the grade), and produces a very strong, hard-wearing joint – which is why it is used in jewellery, where subtlety and strength are so important. It is available in sheets, strips or as a paste in a syringe.

Metals that can be silver-soldered are: steel, silver-steel, brass, copper, nickel-silver, stainless steel, silver, gold and various others. Aluminium and other low-melting-point alloys cannot be silver-soldered.

The process is done on a very simple hearth, often just a cluster of soldering blocks on a soldering sheet (these not only protect and insulate surrounding surfaces, but they also reflect the heat back on to the job being soldered).

Always make sure you have a bucket of water beside you and that there is nothing flammable within a couple of feet of where you are working. Also remember that smoke or heat detectors may be set off unintentionally if you are working near them.

Always turn off the torch as soon as you have finished heating.

The item or area being soldered should be thoroughly cleaned, using wet-and-dry or similar, to bright, shiny metal and then flux applied to the area that you want the silver-solder to flow in. The most common flux is borax powder, and half a thimble full of this or less should be mixed with water to form a creamy paste that can be applied with a brush. The silver-solder can be cut into small pillions – squares 2 or 3mm or so, depending on the size of the job.

One or more pillions are put into the flux, over the joint, and then the torch lit and applied.

For small repairs or making, a small butane torch, such as are also used in the kitchen for crème brûlée, can be used. They are obtainable online very easily and very cheaply, using lighter canisters for refills. Try to buy the type with a self-ignition button.

Heat the joint evenly, making sure both sides get hot. If it is something uneven, like a jump-ring on a pendant, then make sure to apply most of the heat to the larger ring to prevent overheating and possibly melting the small jump-ring. As it gets up to temperature, the workpiece will approach red heat, and you will see the silver-solder start to melt, then liquefy like mercury and flow through the joint. Once it has flowed to where you want it, you can remove the heat and turn the torch off. Solder will always follow the heat when it is liquid, so if you want it to move along, slowly move your torch and the solder will follow (assuming the job is clean and fluxed).

Using silver-solder paste is even easier, as the paste includes its own flux – so all you need do is clean the job, apply paste (making sure it is on both parts) and then heat it. Be warned though, you need to heat the paste in one go – do not take the torch away halfway through and then try and come back to it – it won't work, and you'll need to clean it off again and start over.

After the joint has been made, pick it up from the hearth with a pair of pliers and quench it in water to make it safe. All being well, you will have a very strong, smooth joint that just requires cleaning.

PICKLE

Pickle is a generic term for the chemical used for cleaning the metal after it has been heated by soldering or annealing. Heating brass or similar up to these high temperatures causes a thin layer of scale to form, which is easiest dealt with by chemical cleaning rather than mechanical, such as wet-and-dry paper. The pickle is kept in a 'bath' or a jar that should be sufficient to submerge the work in its entirety. Non-reactive tongs are used to remove the work from the pickle, after which it should be thoroughly rinsed off with water. The work should always be allowed to cool before immersing in any pickle to avoid splashes of acid.

The old-fashioned pickle was a 10 per cent solution of sulphuric acid, which, although highly effective, is not something that most of us would like around the workplace or home. If you are thinking of using such serious chemicals then remember always to add acid to water, and never the other way round, and stir it in as it is being poured to prevent heat build-up.

I always have a jar of pickle handy. Pickle comes in various forms. My favourite is the swimming-pool additive, PH Down, which comes in 1kg tubs from Amazon and suchlike, and half a dozen tablespoonfuls into a large mayonnaise jar of water (clearly labelled, for safety!) creates a very effective cleaning solution. Others prefer citric acid, available from chemists as a food additive, and while not quite as quick at cleaning, it is certainly safer in a mixed environment. Normally,

20 minutes in pickle followed by a thorough rinse under the tap will clean off most of the crud from the soldering. Be warned – do not use the same mix of pickle on silver if you've been using it for brass or copper, or your silver will come out copper coloured!

Like all techniques, good soldering requires some practice, and it is well worth having a little go on things that don't matter first. However, once mastered, it is incredibly useful and very satisfying.

COOL PASTE

Once in a while it is necessary to solder (silver or soft) near other components that will melt or come unstuck when heated. This can be a real pain, and is best avoided where possible by forethought and good sequencing of work. However, it can still happen, even if it's just making a repair.

Help is at hand.

Intended to protect areas not requiring heat when soldering, such as stones, areas of metal or soldered joints, Technoflux Cool Paste can be applied liberally, which will very effectively isolate heat from the area.

The effectiveness of this has been tested by getting a 5cm-long strip of brass, 1cm wide, and very liberally applying this paste all the way round the centre (in a complete ring) and then, holding one end by the fingers, heating the other end up to red heat. It got a little warm, perhaps 40°C. The heat goes into the moisture in the paste and will 'kill' the paste before the heat can travel to the other end, acting as a heat-sink.

This has been used when it was necessary to silver-solder something 30mm away from plastic-centred wheels, and it was safely achieved with no problem. Cool Paste is available from Cooksongold among other suppliers.

It is not suggested in any way that everything should be silver-soldered – far from it – merely that silver-soldering is another tool and technique that can be added to the armoury given its significant usefulness. It is also extremely easy and very satisfying to do. There are many informative videos on YouTube on various aspects of silver-soldering where many hours can be profitably spent.

Suppliers: Cooksongold.com; cupalloys.co.uk

GLUES

It is important, so far as one can, to use the right glue for the job. There are so many different sorts of glue out there, and many have been carefully designed to do specific things or have specific attributes – it helps to be aware of these when making or mending.

This is not intended as an exhaustive list, but simply some of the more common adhesives.

PVA (polyvinyl acetate) – white glue. This is an adhesive for porous materials, such as wood, paper and cloth. Generally it is not water-resistant, although 'waterproof' types are available. It can be watered down, and added to paint, plaster and cement. It is not a 'structural' adhesive, but is very useful within the creative environments.

Copydex – latex dissolved in water, with ammonia added as a stabilizer to the rubber solution. Copydex is a contact adhesive, i.e. you apply it to both surfaces, let it dry and then place them together; very good for fabrics. Like all contact adhesives, care must be taken not to touch two primed surfaces together prematurely, as they will stick and the finish will be damaged pulling them apart. Strength is not great, but it is normally used with a larger surface area.

Cyanoacrylates – superglues, now available in many forms. There are specific types for glass – useful to give an invisible joint and low 'bloom' (the frosting that normal superglues can cause on glass). Other common variables include the viscosity – runny or gel – and the speed of setting.

Cyanoacrylates are very good at sticking to most things – wood, metals, fabrics, glass, ceramics and most plastics – but won't cope well with polyethylene, polypropylene or PTFE. Generally, they struggle with temperature as well, so around 80°C is the limit – don't mend your tea mug with it!

Epoxy resins – again there are many types, including structural adhesives. For making, we have two distinct types – the 5min type and the 24hr type.

Five-minute epoxy (and the 90sec type) are fast-acting, two-part adhesives that come either in a double syringe or in two tubes. When mixed, you have a short time to apply and locate the parts, holding them in position till they set. Compared to the alternatives, they are not high-strength and have a minute amount of flexibility, even when cured. They are fine for applying 'decoration' but not for serious holding strength, such as a repair. The best that I have found in this category is Devcon High Strength 5 Minute, which is significantly stronger than most found in DIY chains.

The 24hr epoxies are stronger, having longer to cure and create more chemical bonds – and are, therefore, better used when strength is the priority.

Milliput Epoxy Putty – is an extremely useful material curing rock-hard in around 4hrs, and fully curing in about twice that. It is supplied in two 'bars', which when mixed thoroughly together in equal quantities can be handled like plasticene. When cured, it can be machined, tapped and drilled, sanded and painted. Milliput can be used for making small items, repairs, gap-filling or a multitude of other uses.

1
HATS

INTRODUCTION AND HISTORY

The term milliner originally meant 'using goods from Milan', which included gloves, buttons and small accessories. This somehow changed in the eighteenth century to mean making head-coverings and the current term was born.

Hats can be made from any material, including all the dressmaking fabrics (some having been millinery stiffened) buckram, straw and even wood. Hats are used for protection, as in the case of sun and bee-keepers' hats, riding and builders' hard hats. Also, for identification, as in the case of military hats, policemen, chefs, royalty and, more than anything, for completing a fashionable outfit.

Medieval and Before

Hats were used a lot for protection and, in the forming of the religious orders, head coverings became a strong requirement for devotion in many religions. Some of these ecclesiastically born hats were redesigned for common use. With the emergence of the Renaissance period (1300 to 1600), many head coverings would be individually wrapped or made, impossible to know exactly, so here are a few typical worn hats.

MEN'S FASHIONS
The Phrygian Cap
The Phrygian hat came to Britain from Europe and can be seen from as early as the first millennium. It is a 'pull-on' cap with a curved shape on the top. They were usually made in two pieces and could be made from leather, wool or linen. They were brought back into fashion many times in the following millennia and also came to symbolize 'freedom and the pursuit of liberty' during the American Civil War and French Revolution, when they were called liberty caps.

Sectioned Caps
Short, multi-sectioned caps, fitted to the head, were worn for protection and also for devotion.

Coifs
Men wore hoods, often with a small shoulder cape attached. The hood section was made with two pieces, resulting in a corner at the top; this was called the 'liripipe'. The liripipe became a focus of fashion and gradually lengthened in the fourteenth century; it continued to lengthen until it became impractical to wear and was rolled round the hood. The end of the liripipe was worn under the chin and tucked into the folds of the rolls. This hat was then refashioned into a hat in its own right and was called a chaperon.

WOMEN'S FASHIONS
Barbette/Wimple/Veil
Religious orders rejected all types of flirtation, including the showing of hair, and nuns would, therefore, wear a combination of a barbette, wimple and veil. These items were brought into the fashion arena and adapted. The barbette was a chin strap, which was put on first, the wimple then was worn over the head and sat round the chin, often by way of shaped fabric with a hole for the head to go through, the veil then went over this and was held on with either clips or a circlet.

A	Wimple.	O	Beaver with buckle for mid-seventeenth-century Puritan.
B	Barbette.		
C	Hood with liripipe.	P	Tricorn hat.
D	Henin with butterfly veil.	Q	Bicorn hat.
E	Phrygian hat.	R	Fontange.
F	Crispinette, shown attached to a roundel.	S	Poke bonnet.
G	Chaperon.	T	Calash.
H	Fifteenth-century flat cap.	U	Smaller Victorian bonnet.
I	Elizabethan cap.	V	Top hat.
J	Gable hood.	W	Bowler hat.
K	French hood.	X	Boater.
L	Copotain.	Y	Panama.
M	Linen cap.	YY	Cloche hat.
N	Beaver, turned up for seventeenth-century Cavaliers.	Z	Trilby.
		ZZ	Baseball cap.

Crispinette
The crispinette covered the side of the head and in the thirteenth century this was quite plain, though sometimes meshed. During the fourteenth century, it became more decorative and in the fifteenth century, the crispinette developed further to create wide cylinders on either side of the head. The veils became more elaborate, and it could also be worn with jewelled crowns or circlets.

Henin
The conical henins of Europe were not worn much in Britain, though a form of henin that was worn was flattened on the top and worn with a veil. Sometimes the veil was held away from the hat with wires – this was called a butterfly veil.

Sixteenth Century

MEN'S FASHIONS
Although plain hoods were still worn by many working men, the fashion encouraged a smaller, soft-brimmed cap. The hats were made from fur felt, straw or brocade, often to match the outfit worn.

Petasos
The petasos (originally from Greece) was a wide-brimmed felt hat. The crown was usually small and fitted to the head and the hat was used for travelling. Monks and priests might also wear a petasos when out among the people.

Tudor Cap
The Tudor cap had a soft crown, gathered into a soft brim. In the sixteenth century, the brim might have been 'dagged' and turned up on to the crown. The brim later became smooth and smaller, and sat horizontally. The crown further developed into a shaped pattern with a flat top and side panels, which sat down on to the brim. The style endured into, and through, the next century.

Capotain (Copotain)
The capotain arrived from Italy towards the end of the sixteenth century. It was a hard, conical hat with a stiff brim and could be made from fur felt or stiffened brocade. It was fashionable throughout the Elizabethan era and was probably the forerunner to the top hat.

WOMEN'S FASHIONS
The henin endured for a while into the sixteenth century. Women were still covering their hair, though this changed with a further development of the wimple and veil, and later during Elizabeth I's reign, women started wearing what we would call hats, first with a smaller version of the men's capotain hat. By the end of Elizabeth I's reign, women were showing a lot of hair and covering as little as possible, with tiny hats perched on top.

The Gable Hood
The gable hood was essentially an English invention. An embroidered, stiff, front hood was developed in the shape of a gable roof, with a non-structural drape on the back and long lappets falling from behind. A small cap was worn under the gable for stability and the drape fell around the shoulders. The hood became more structural through the century with further rings of embroidered bands behind the gable front.

The French Hood
During Henry VIII's reign, the gable hood was periodically changed for a French hood. This allowed some hair to be shown and was a much softer shape at the front, sometimes hugging the head and sometimes with a wired, sweeping shape at the front. The front shape was to endure into Elizabeth I's reign and was favoured by Mary Queen of Scots, though Elizabeth lost the drape at the back.

Seventeenth Century

Felt hats came into their own during this century. The century was politically charged and changes happened quickly with the Commonwealth in 1649, followed by the Restoration of the monarchy in 1669.

MEN'S FASHIONS

The Beaver

Made with beaver, this was a wide-crowned, wide-brimmed hat. During this century, it went through a few changes: the brim became wider, it was turned up on one side and trimmed with feathers. During the Commonwealth, the crown was also reshaped to resemble the capotain of the previous centuries and adorned with a band and a buckle worn by the Puritans. The Cavaliers still wore the decorated version and further embellished it.

The Tricorn

Towards the end of the century, there was a further development of the beaver: the wide brim was turned up on three sides, forming a triangular hat with three points. This style was to endure until the end of the following century.

WOMEN'S FASHIONS

For the most part, women would wear a smaller version of the men's fashions, small linen caps or the caps from the previous century without the drapes at the back; now women were at liberty to show their hair.

During the Commonwealth, the Puritan women would cover their hair – a more pious look being more acceptable. These would be plain linen, often with a starched band at the front.

Eighteenth Century

MEN'S FASHIONS

During the 1700s, the tricorn hat endured throughout. They were usually fur felt hats and black, though there were lighter colours for the more adventurous. The hats were more tailored to shape now and often decorated with feathers. The military also took on the tricorn and added cockades of ribbons and feathers. The tricorn hat was worn by all classes, naturally with a varying amount of decoration.

The large-brimmed hats were still favoured by some, while clergy favoured low-crowned, flat-brimmed hats.

The Bicorn

Towards the end of the century, the tricorn was re-formed into a bicorn. The back and the front of the hats were turned up, with the two points sitting at the sides.

The Top Hat

A form of top hat started to be seen at the end of the century.

WOMEN'S FASHIONS

Women were still perching tiny hats on their ever-rising hairstyles and with the larger hairstyles came larger hats to accommodate them.

Fontange (Frelange)

At the end of the previous century, a fashion came from Europe that was usually called commode in England. It consisted of a wire-framed and lace-covered high fan that stood high from the front of the hair, and a cap that covered some of the hair at the back. The fontange was sometimes made with a starched fabric, folded into a fan. As with most fashions, it eventually became impractical and died out early in the century.

Calash

This was a large hood, often attached to a travelling cape. It was developed to cover and protect the huge hairstyles of the period. To do this, large wire or cane ribs were inserted in several places through the hood.

Nineteenth Century

Hairstyles and fashion, generally, became a little more sombre in the 1800s. The bicorn disappeared and hats that we are more familiar with became fashionable.

The Top Hat

The beaver, as it was still called, went through many styles through the nineteenth century. In the early years, it was a large, very shapely hat with the brim curving down at the front and back. At the same time, a very tall hat was seen, called the 'stovepipe': it was made of silk velvet, which gave it a high sheen. The tall crown quickly became shorter and, towards the end of the century, it developed the slight shape to the crown and the practical top hat was born – a fashion that endured throughout the following centuries for formal occasions.

Deerstalker

A multi-sectioned cap with a small peak and flaps that could be tied up at the sides was introduced for hunting. It was made from tweed and was first seen in the middle of the century.

Bowler

A further development of the capotain of the previous centuries was a hard-topped bowler hat, which originally was used as protective wear for riding and labouring, though it became part of the livery of many office-based workers. First seen in the 1880s, the original ones had a higher crown and the brim was more shaped than the twentieth-century development.

Boater

A hard straw hat also made its appearance in the latter half of the nineteenth century. Originally a fashion item, it became a uniform for many gentle sports and schools. The boaters were so hard, they were generally made bespoke to the shape of the man's head.

The Flat Cap

A cap with a brim, which, instead of the multi-sectioned shape, had a flat top with soft sides; it was very popular with the working classes. It also became fashionable with some sports, including golf.

Homburg

Another hat that originated as a hunting hat was the homburg, a stiffer felt hat with a small, flat brim with a sharp turnover at the edge and a crease down the top.

WOMEN'S FASHIONS

The Bonnet

There were many forms of bonnet during this century. It was very popular, at the start of the 1800s, to secure a hat on the head with a scarf or length of fabric tied under the chin. This might have been an adaption of a man's hat; however, it quickly developed into the bonnet. The poke bonnet was formed, which had a small crown and a very deep brim coming forward to obscure the face, usually made from braided straw. By the 1830, the brim had opened right out and was lined with all kinds of beautiful embroidery and draped silk. Through the 1830s, large ribbon and silk flower decorations adorned the bonnet and the brim swept down lower at the sides to allow more room for this. It might have been made from buckram, straw or stiffened linen. The 1840s saw the brim becoming part of the crown, developing an almost cylindrical shape. From this point, the bonnet became smaller, so that by the 1880s, it was very small, perching on the back of the head.

The Round Hat

During the 1860s, the round hat was very popular. This consisted of a very small crown and a large brim, and was usually made from braided straw. It might have been tied on with a scarf, if travelling, or shaped down at the front and the back. Smaller versions of it were taken up in the uniforms of schools, resembling the boaters of the men's fashions.

Twentieth Century

MEN'S FASHIONS

The hats from the end of the previous century were still popular – the homburg, boater, deerstalker and caps – and they all played a part throughout this century too. The top hat was still popular with the elite and on celebration days.

Trilby

The trilby hat took many forms and is still popular today. A softer-styled hat with a flat brim and dent in the crown, folded down the centre and forming a holding pattern at the front, it was popular with all classes. A smaller brim and slightly pulled up at the back was popular with musicians. The trilby could be made from felt, tweed, straw or a synthetic material.

Pork Pie Hat

This has a flat top, a strong indent around the top and a small, upturned brim; it was a popular street hat and especially popular in the 1960s.

Panama Hat

This hat was introduced from Europe in the nineteenth century and was especially popular toward the end of that century and into the twentieth, through to the 1930s and beyond, as a summer hat. It comes in a variety of brim widths and is not unlike the trilby, though it has a straighter crown with a teardrop dent in the top. They are often made from woven straw.

Baseball Cap

This cap was worn for sport since the mid-nineteenth century, but came on to the streets during the 1940s and has become very commonplace ever since. The size and shape of the peak, and method of fastening at the back of the crown, are of high fashion importance and change regularly.

Beanie Hat (Skullies)

The beanie hat, a knitted, head-hugging, wool or acrylic hat came from America in the early 1900s. It has been worn for warmth by everyone for winter sports and outside work. It has changed little and is sometimes lined for extra warmth. It can either be designer branded or made by hand at home.

WOMEN'S FASHIONS

Again, at the start of the century, women might wear smaller versions of the men's hats; in particular, a small trilby or homburg might be worn. However, once hairstyles became large, so the hats followed suit.

The Driving Cap

With the use of the car being more commonplace, a large crowned, peaked cap, resembling the tam o'shanter hat of the Scottish fashions became popular. It was worn with a large, silk chiffon scarf covering the hair and face for protection from the elements.

Feathers and Birds

Before the First World War, brimmed hats became more lavish and they had wide crowns to accommodate the wide hair fashions. Towards the 1910s, they became more shaped and the decorations became more amazing. Sometimes whole stuffed birds were perched on the hat or huge ribbon decorations.

Torque and Cloche

The war brought a major change and large torques, taken from nurses' uniforms, were sometimes worn, pulled down over the ears. The cloche was introduced and worn throughout the 1920s. It could be worn tight to the head or pulled out to a small brim. A cloche with a brim made wider at the sides, shaped downward round the sides of the face, was also worn.

1930s to the 1960s

The hat was extremely popular during this time and a very wide range was available from the

'Florentine', which had a high, tapered crown, to the sailor's hat and also wide-brimmed hats for summer days and holidays. The Second World War brought more sombre looks and the 1940s brought a more tailored look with many felt hats, shaped to the head with folds and stiff shapes, including a matador hat. The 1950s were a little more frivolous, with feathers and flowers adorning the headwear, and were worn almost as part of the hairstyles of the day. In the 1960s, hats had a last blast of popularity with loud colours, large multi-sectioned hats, rain hats and, for formal wear, the netted pillbox hat.

Fascinators
The fascinator, a small hat or hair decoration, often made from sinemay or crinoline, became popular in the 1960s for occasional wear. Sinemay is very malleable and many outrageous shapes can be formed from it. The fascinator continues to be seen at weddings and formal occasions.

Hats since this have changed little, for any style, slightly changed by fashion or one's personal taste, can be worn as a personal expression.

PROJECT 1 THE STRAW RIBBON BONNET

Straw was a very popular way of making hats in the eighteenth and nineteenth centuries, both for men and women. Straw can be woven into many widths and densities and can be stiffened, as in the case of the straw boater, or be left soft, as in the case of many bonnets. You can buy straight braids of straw or lace edging, both of which are used in this example. Straw ribbon also comes in many colours or can be dyed.

There are dedicated sewing-machines for stitching straw braid, which, of course, would be quicker and easier to use; however, this demonstration shows that, with care, it is quite achievable to make one on a domestic machine with the minimum of equipment. It is not a long process and it is quite possible to make the main part of the bonnet with a few hours' work.

These bonnets can be lined with silk and the possibilities are endless when it comes to decorations, but this example demonstrates the main skills required to make the hat.

Materials Required

- 20m of green 10mm straw ribbon.
- 50cm of 30mm natural colour, lace straw ribbon.
- Ribbon or braid to decorate.
- A former or hat block on which to mould the bonnet into shape.
- A braiding machine foot (it is possible to sew the bonnet without this but it is very helpful to keep the ribbon evenly sewn).

The Pattern

In this case, the pattern is made by eye and to the hat block or former that has been chosen.

- First, measure the head of the person for whom the hat is intended. Measurement should be taken round the head in the position and angle that the hat will sit.
- Find a hat block for this size. If the block is too small, it can be bound with fabric to increase the size. This former can equally be a kitchen bowl or anything that is the desired shape. If the former is porous, first cover it in cling film or thin plastic.
- Draw out the design so you have something to refer to when making the bonnet.

Order of Work

The bonnet will be started from the centre back and worked outwards. The ribbon will be sewn under the preceding row.

1. Take the main braid, carefully roll it up and soak it in lukewarm water for approximately 10min; this will make it more malleable, both for stretching and bending the ribbon, as shown in Fig. 1.3.
2. To start the stitching, turn over the end of the ribbon and gently curl the ribbon round and under the end.
3. Adjust the slider on the machine foot to ensure that the ribbon will be caught by the stitching on the way round (only 7–8mm of the braid should be seen from the right side of the bonnet).
4. Work your way round in a spiral, pushing the ribbon towards the machine foot and carefully bending it round to ensure you get a flat piece of work.
5. Measure the plate (ribbon already worked) against your former and continue until it reaches the point when it should curve round.
6. Now angle the plate upwards (see Fig. 1.5) and pull the braid as it enters the machine; this will bring the crown of the bonnet round.
7. Once you have the desired depth of the crown, turn the hat so that the side you have been stitching is on the outside and start pushing the braid again and angling the crown up to allow the form to straighten out again.

Fig. 1.1 Straight straw braid and lace braid.

Fig. 1.2 Soak the braid in warm water.

Fig. 1.3 Note how much more malleable the braid is.

8. At this point, decide the back of the bonnet and start taking the ribbon under the previous line and cut, as shown in Fig. 1.6.

9. Resume the stitching by bringing the ribbon from under the previous row and around the crown. This will form a cut-out in the back of the bonnet to allow for a bun, or comfort round the neck.

TIP

Using a large stitch with a very slight zigzag will limit the chance of cutting through the straw and allow a slight stretching of the hat, if it is necessary. The zigzag stitch should not be enough to show as a zigzag.

Fig. 1.4 Sew the braid under the previous row.

Fig. 1.5 Turn the plate up and stretch the braid slightly to curve the crown.

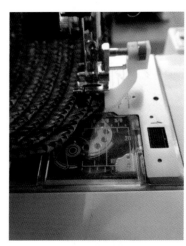

Fig. 1.6 Tuck the braid under the previous row.

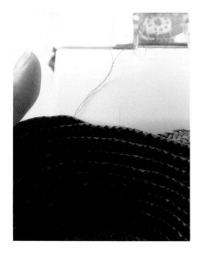

Fig. 1.7 Start the row again 2cm further on.

Fig. 1.8 The finished crown.

Fig. 1.9 The graduated back.

Fig. 1.10 Neaten the inside.

Fig. 1.11 Start tipping the bonnet and ease the braid in to flatten the brim.

Fig. 1.12 Build on the brim.

ADDING IN MORE RIBBON

If you run out of braid, finish off the end in the same way as shown in Fig. 1.6, then start a new piece of braid front under this end.

10. Again, finish the row by tipping the ribbon under the previous row, matching up with the previously finished row.

11. Continue like this for eight rows, creating an arch in the back to allow for a bun or ringlets of the wearer.

12. For the brim of the bonnet, make several flat rows (in this case ten), starting 8cm away from the edge and finishing likewise on the other side, as shown in Figs 1.13, 1.14, 1.15 and 1.16.

13. When finished, cut the ends into a curve, as shown in Fig. 1.16.

14. Stitch another piece of ribbon around the end, along the front of the brim and round the other end, this time on the front of the brim (this will allow the lace-straw ribbon to cover the cut

Fig. 1.13 Begin the lappet sides
of the bonnet.

Fig. 1.14 Continue the brim,
ensuring it is sitting flat.

Fig. 1.15 Stretch the final row to allow
a slight curve inwards to the edge.

Fig. 1.16 Trim off the end
of each lappet.

Fig. 1.17 Neaten the cut edge with
another row.

Fig. 1.18 Bend the same braid round
the front of the bonnet.

ends). When stitching this row, pull the ribbon gently to create a slight curve inwards to the brim (this will add a bit of character to the hat).

15. Take the lace-straw ribbon and sew this with two rows of stitching to the inside of the bonnet, encasing the ends as you do (Fig 1.19).

16. Tidy up the edges of the braid on the inside of the hat with stitches and some fabric fray – glue.

17. Finally, decorate the hat as desired with braid and silk ribbons. Stitch some long lengths of silk ribbon from the indented areas of the bonnet.

18. The bonnet should sit well on the head. However, if it is imbalanced, it may be necessary to add a comb to the inside front of the bonnet.

Fig. 1.19 Sew the lace under the last row.

Fig. 1.20 The shape of the bonnet without decoration.

Fig. 1.21 Add ribbon trim.

Fig. 1.22 The finished bonnet.

PROJECT 2 MAKING POLYSTYRENE HAT BLOCKS

Wooden hat-blocks are, of course, the best equipment to block felt hats, though they are expensive and if you are not going to take the art up as professional, you may like to see how to make hat blocks out of polystyrene. The polystyrene has to be high density and it is important that you take the time to get a good finish to the block.

The polystyrene blocks are surprisingly robust, though they will need replacing eventually. Make sure you cover them with cling film when using for felt blocking.

> **NOTE**
>
> The blocks shown here are for a head size of 60cm. You will need to size up or down from here by increasing the circumference. It is important to note that with the shaping of the polystyrene, the size usually becomes slightly smaller, so it is possible that this pattern could finish as small as 58cm, depending on how keen you are with the rasp.

Materials Required

- Cubes of high-density polystyrene to cover the size of the hat block you want to make (for the trilby shown, (HxWxL) 40 × 40 × 50cm for the crown.
- Various tools for the carving, including sharp cutting tools such as a large blade or sharp bread-knife.
- Small rasps are useful for rounding and digging shapes.
- Files for gully cutting.
- Different grades of abrasive paper.
- Either some 18mm ply or MDF for the base of the block.

The Pattern

You can use the pattern provided for the trilby crown, though much of the shaping is by eye. Find a hat that you want to make and compare the hat from each elevation. Take measurements or photos and refer to them continually. The blocks for the brim are very much carved by eye, using the same techniques; study the shape of the hat you want to make the brim for and adapt the measurements to your requirements.

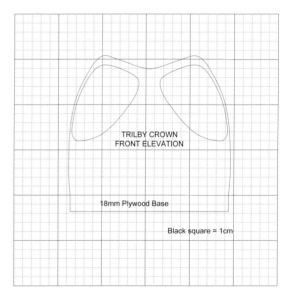

TRILBY CROWN
FRONT ELEVATION

18mm Plywood Base

Black square = 1cm

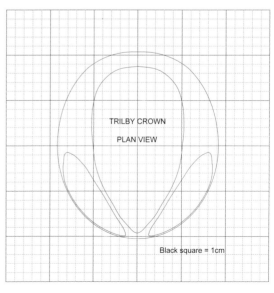

TRILBY CROWN

PLAN VIEW

Black square = 1cm

Collection of blocks.

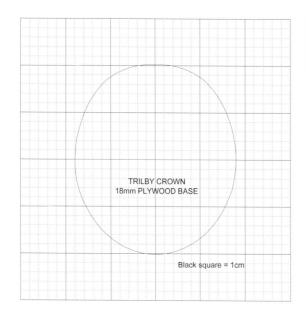

TRILBY CROWN
18mm PLYWOOD BASE

Black square = 1cm

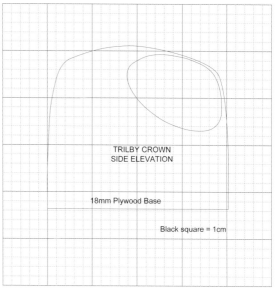

TRILBY CROWN
SIDE ELEVATION

18mm Plywood Base

Black square = 1cm

Order of Work

THE CROWN

1. Take the square block and draw the oval shape of the pattern on the top and bottom, as shown in Fig. 1.24.
2. Gradually cut the polystyrene into a straight column shape. Do this slowly, carving a small amount off at a time, as shown in Fig. 1.25, to avoid over-cutting or breakages.
3. Smooth the column with the rasp. Move the rasp round the piece in smooth motions to get an equally smooth finish.
4. Smooth the column a little with some sandpaper to help the next stage, as shown in Fig. 1.27.
5. Draw the shapes required on to the top of the column (Fig. 1.28).
6. Draw a line around the column to the point (approximately halfway down the block). This is the point where you do not want to cut beyond, because the head needs to fit into it.

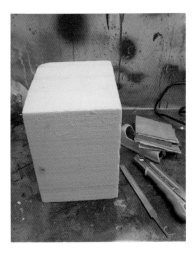

Fig. 1.23 The original block, cut to size.

Fig. 1.24 Mark the oval head size on top and bottom.

Fig. 1.25 Carefully carve the curves.

Fig. 1.26 Smooth with a file.

Fig. 1.27 Further smooth with sandpaper.

Fig. 1.28 Mark the other shaping patterns on the block.

7. To ensure that you cut evenly, cut further lines around the column and cut slowly to get the roundness of the shape (you can always take more away; adding on is more difficult!). This process is shown below.

8. Draw any further indents or creases that you need and carve these away carefully. You may find a small rasp helps in this process.

9. You should now have the desired shape to the block.

10. Finish the shape off with abrasive paper of ever decreasing grades. The smoother you can get the block, the more effective it will be.

11. Cut the base of the block out of the ply or MDF, the same shape as the base of the block you have just made, and drill a 2.5cm hole in the centre.

12. Carve or drill out a corresponding hole around 8cm deep in the centre bottom of the polystyrene and then stick the ply and polystyrene together with PVA glue (do not use a spirit-based glue as this will melt the polystyrene and ruin all your good work).

Fig. 1.29 Start shaping evenly round the block.

Fig. 1.30 Work from the first two tramlines.

Fig. 1.31 Work from the second to third line.

Fig. 1.32 Start creating the top dip.

Fig. 1.33 Work into the dip with the rasp.

Fig. 1.34 Start work on the side creases.

Fig. 1.35 Continue on the top.

Fig. 1.36 Look at the overall shape continuously to ensure an even look.

Fig. 1.37 Smooth the side creases with sandpaper.

Fig. 1.38 Use finer abrasive paper to further smooth.

Fig. 1.39 Cut a wooden base and stick on with PVA glue.

Fig. 1.40 The finished crown block.

NOTE

The wooden base will prolong the life of the block and help in the blocking of the hats. The block can be placed on a head block holder and used as a brace to pull on the felt hoods. The wood can also be used for pinning into, which will also lengthen the life of the block.

THE BRIM OF THE HAT

1. The brim of the hat is made in the same way as the crown. Draw on the desired width (Fig. 1.41).
2. Carefully cut this out into a column, as shown in Fig. 1.42. Even out the shape with the rasp and check the size and shape by placing the crown on the top.

NOTE

The base that you are carving is carved 'up-side down' to allow for the felt to go into the polystyrene, with an unturned flange, so you won't be able to get an exact comparison of the shape.

3. Draw around the crown block and draw on the top of the brim block the areas that need to be carved into an angle (Fig. 1.44).
4. Cut out the centre oval and smooth this with abrasive paper.

5. The brim will need an indent all the way around at the correct angle to finish off the shape of the brim, as shown in Figs 1.45 and 1.46. This will allow the felt to be anchored well, at the same time as tipping over the edge of the brim, giving it a professional look.
6. Finish off the block in the same way as the crown, with ever higher grades of abrasive paper, until it is smooth.
7. Cut some ply or MDF in the same shape as the base of the brim and stick together with PVA glue.

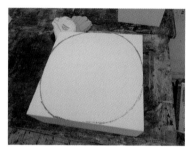

Fig. 1.41 Mark the outer shape on to the brim block.

Fig. 1.42 Cut out the brim shape evenly.

Fig. 1.43 Offer up to the crown block to ensure the required size and shape.

Fig. 1.44 Mark on the block the required shape.

Fig. 1.45 When the required shape is completed, create a gully around the edge at the point of the edge of the brim.

Fig. 1.46 Showing the shape of the trilby block from the side.

Fig. 1.47 Showing the trilby block from the top.

PROJECT 3 FELT BLOCKING

Materials Required

- Suitably sized and shapes of hat blocks. The pattern given for the crown is appropriate for a 60cm head.
- Suitably moulded felt shapes (see each project description).
- 2.5cm milliner's petersham for decoration and inner edging.
- A small amount of lining material (optional).
- Felt stiffener and thinner for diluting or brush cleaning.
- 2.5cm brush for applying stiffener.
- Milliner's wire or edging reed for shaping edge of hat.
- Matching thread and millinery needles.

DONOR FELT

Felt is made from the interlocking fibres of wool, sometimes blended with animal fur and synthetic fibres. Synthetic felts are not appropriate for felt blocking, but are made for other craft work. The felt fabric, when wet can be shaped by stretching and shrinking on to a shaped block. The hats may also be stiffened in order to keep the shape, and in some cases, protect the head.

Although it is possible to shape felt from a flat piece of felt, when making bespoke hats most milliners will buy ready-formed shapes – the most common ones are hoods, flares and capelines – and shape the hat from there.

FELT STIFFENERS

The stiffener most commonly used is spirit-based and tends to give the best results, though a more environmentally friendly, water-based stiffener is available. It is more likely to lead to staining and is more difficult to apply evenly, though it is definitely a viable alternative. If you are short of money and time, you can also use diluted PVA glue; this is even more temperamental but has been used successfully, if you are careful.

STEAM GENERATORS

In order to shape the felts, it is necessary to wet them. The more controlled way of doing this is to apply steam into the hood until the felt is thoroughly, and evenly, damp. This takes some time and often needs to be re-applied because the felt will dry out during manipulation. It is also possible to soak the felt in hot water and then shape it, using steam when necessary. It is important to be careful not to ruin the quality of the felt surface while doing this.

There are millinery attachments that go with the upright garment steamers, which work very well as the hood can be placed over the generator while it is steaming. There are also hand-held steamers, which may take a little longer but are more likely to be around smaller workrooms. Kettles have also been known to be used, though the old-fashioned stove kettles work best, as they can be boiled continually without the automatic shut off.

HAT BLOCK

Traditional hat blocks are made of wood and are available from any good millinery suppliers. However, there is an art to making good ones and, for this reason, they can be expensive. Cheaper alternatives are available:

- You could make a polystyrene hat block, as shown in the previous project; these work well, though last a limited time.
- Most hats can be made using a head-shaped block. Any folds and creases can be added by hand after it has been removed from the block, so investing in one wooden, plain block or a combination block including different crown shapes, would be an economical choice.

BLOCKING PINS

Blocking pins are readily available and come in different sizes and lengths. The traditional ones have easy-to-push ends, though strong household pins are also often used. If this is the case, a push tool is advisable, especially if you are using

A selection of hats made by Katie Kelson, Jade Littlechild, Marika Cholmondeley and Diane Favell.

the wooden hat blocks. If you are using polystyrene blocks, long dressmaker's pins tend to stay in better.

Order of Work

Of the four hats shown here, two are fully blocked and two are blocked and folded, or manipulated on the block. We shall first look at the fully blocked hats.

The Trilby and Bowler

For both hats, use a hood for the crown and a capeline for the brim. Prepare the hat blocks by covering in clingfilm to protect the block and lengthen its life.

THE CROWN

1. Select a suitably sized block for the crown and brim.
2. It is usual to stiffen the felt before blocking, though not essential; stiffening will help retain a defined shape to the hat.

Stiffening
Turn the hood inside out and place on the block. The stiffener may either be sprayed on to the hood or worked into the felt with a brush; work the stiffener in using a circular motion. If you are using the non-spirit-based stiffener, it might be best to spray to prevent it leaking through to the other side of the felt. Leave the hood to dry either overnight or in a drying cabinet, if you have one. The stiffener may be diluted using the thinner (or water in the case of water-based products). The less strong the stiffener, the less stiff the resulting hat will be. The thinner can also be used for cleaning the brushes.

> **TIP**
>
> If the stiffener has bled on to the right side, you may be able to disguise it by brushing gently with a wire brush. You can also use the thinner to clean it or hairspray can also help to take it off the surface.

3. When the hood is dry, turn through to the right side.
4. Hold the hood over steam for a minute or two to allow the steam to penetrate the felt.
5. Place the hood over the block and pull from opposite sides until the top of the hood is flat to the block. This may take a lot of effort but it is worth taking the time to get it on to the block well. If the felt stops stretching, you may place it in the steam again and continue.
6. Work the felt until it is smoothly shaped around the block. You may put a loop of elastic around the block and work it down. Pin the felt low down on the block to avoid marking the hat when it has dried.
7. If your block has indents, as in the case of the trilby, there are many ways of keeping the felt in the shapes. One way is to make stuffed shapes and then pin in place. Professionally, there would be a positive wooden block that would fit into the indents, as shown in Figs 1.54, 1.55 and 1.56.
8. Leave to dry.
9. Decide on the height of the crown and mark around the felt. Cut on this line.
10. Mark the centre front and centre back of the crown.
11. Remove the crown from the block.
12. Leave to dry.

> **TIP**
>
> It might be hard to get the felt off the block. Using a fine strip of metal will help. A corset bone lends itself to the job well.

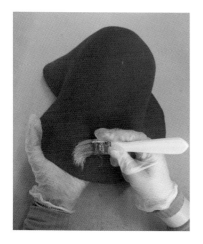

Fig. 1.48 Stiffen the hat with a circular motion.

Fig. 1.49 Hold in the steam until the steam is well absorbed.

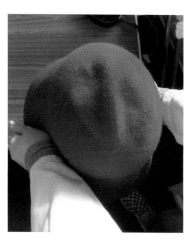

Fig. 1.50 Pull hard from opposite sides on to the block.

Fig. 1.51 Wear gloves to protect your hands from the size.

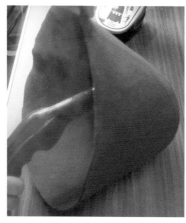

Fig. 1.52 Be careful to keep your hands away from the steam source.

Fig. 1.53 Extra help from a friend is useful to steam and stretch at the same time.

Fig. 1.54 Help the felt into the grooves of the trilby block with your hands first.

Fig. 1.55 Make some pads to hold the grooves in place.

Fig. 1.56 Pin pads in place and mark the height of the crown.

Fig. 1.57 Re-steam when necessary.

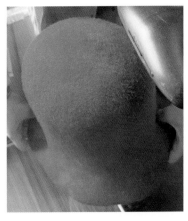

Fig. 1.58 Work the hat until you have a smooth finish.

Fig. 1.59 The sides can be helped down with elastic or cord.

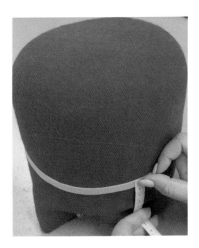

Fig. 1.60 Mark the point where you want the crown to finish.

Fig. 1.61 Removing the crown from the block using a corset steel.

Fig. 1.62 The finished trilby crown by Katie Kelson.

THE BRIM OF THE HAT

1. The brim of the hat is worked in the same way. After stiffening and steaming the capeline, place it right side up on to the brim block and work the inner edge. Pin in place.
2. Stretch the brim over the outside edge and down to the groove, which defines the edge of the brim.
3. The felt should be worked into this groove. This can be done using cord and a milliner's knot, which can be tightened into the groove. You can see how to tie a milliner's knot below.
4. Leave to dry.
5. Mark a line on the inside of the brim, 15mm into the inner hole.
6. Mark the centre front and centre back of the brim.
7. Cut around the outside edge of the felt before removing from the block.
8. It is best to check the size of the hat at this point, before sewing in the petersham, which doesn't stretch. If the hat is too small, it is possible to stretch the hat slightly by applying more steam and pushing it on to a large head form – or even your head – until it fits well.
9. Cut and stab-stitch the petersham to the inner side of the brim.

Fig. 1.63 Showing the process of blocking the brim.

Fig. 1.64 Hold the felt in the groove using cord and a milliner's knot.

Fig. 1.65 The blocked bowler hat brim.

Fig. 1.66 It takes a while to get a smooth finish.

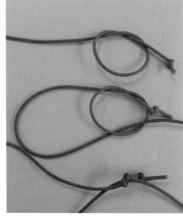

Fig. 1.67 Showing a millinery knot.

Fig. 1.68 Trim the brim to follow a good curve.

Fig. 1.69 Buttonhole stitch the wire in place. The wire can be pulled gently to further enhance the curve of the brim.

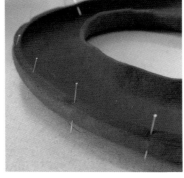

Fig. 1.70 Pin the petersham, folded over the edge, and stab-stitch through.

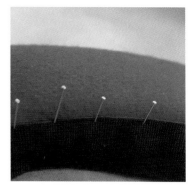

Fig. 1.71 Stab-stitch petersham in place.

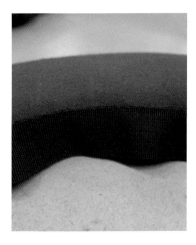

Fig. 1.72 Make small stitches as invisible as possible.

Fig. 1.73 The wire is sewn 1cm inside the edge.

Fig. 1.74 Turn the edge over and stab-stitch.

Fig. 1.75 Make sure you do not make the hat small as you put the petersham in.

Fig. 1.76 The petersham in place.

> **TIP**
>
> Petersham always sits better, whether sewing to the inside or outside of the hat, if it is slightly curved. You can do this using an iron. Hold the petersham in a curve on the ironing board and pass a steam iron over the petersham – you will find it curves well.

Finishing the Edge

1. Decide exactly where the edge will be. In the case of the bowler, this will be beyond the turn-up of the felt. Mark this line and measure some millinery wire to fit, including a crossover. In the case of the trilby, this wire should be stitched 1cm from the edge, on the top of the brim. The bowler should have the wire sewn on to the edge of the hat. The wire should be sewn on using blanket stitch.
2. The edge of the trilby hat should not be turned over the wire. It should be stab-stitched in place very carefully and neatly.
3. The bowler brim will be covered in petersham and stab-stitched through. Be aware that the quality of the stitching will define the look of the finished hat.

ATTACHING THE BRIM TO THE CROWN

1. Place the front and back marking together and place the crown over the brim lip.
2. Stab-stitch the two felts together, behind the petersham.

3. Add any decoration to the hat; traditionally on a bowler and trilby, this would be a petersham or silk ribbon with a flat bow on the side (on the left side for a man's hat, right for a lady), though the choice is yours.

Fig. 1.77 The finished bowler by Jade Littlechild.

Fig. 1.78 A flat bow in place.

Fig. 1.78a The finished trilby.

Manipulated Hats

The two hats shown below are made using a capeline and hood. The black hat was steamed, while the cloche was soaked in hot water after stiffening and before blocking.

1. Turn the felt inside out and apply the stiffener in the same way as previously.
2. Leave to dry.

3. The cloche is now fully submerged in hot water and partially dried by pressing between towels (avoid squeezing as this will affect the surface of the felt).
4. Both hats are now steamed and stretched over the block.
5. Mark the place to be folded by pinning tape around the hat.
6. Pull the felt up to the line. The fold may be sharpened using an iron (and more steam).

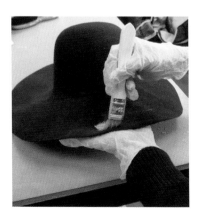

Fig. 1.79 The capeline being stiffened.

Fig. 1.80 Decide on the depth of the crown and mark.

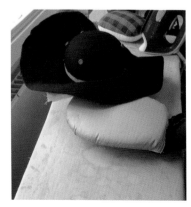

Fig. 1.81 Pull the brim up to the required point.

Fig. 1.82 A damp cloth and iron may also be used.

Fig. 1.83 Soak the hood in hot water.

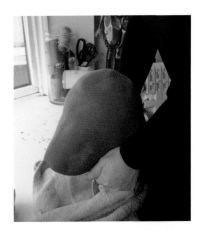

Fig. 1.84 Pull over a form to get the top flat and pulled in down the sides.

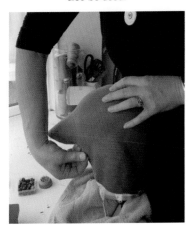

Fig. 1.85 Pin the neck edge closely to keep smooth while working the rest of the hat.

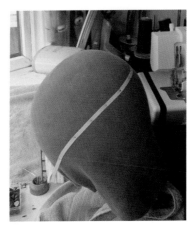

Fig. 1.86 Mark where to place the first fold.

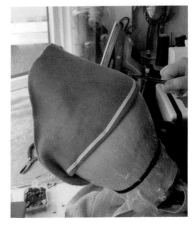

Fig. 1.87 Fold up and hold in place.

BLACK HAT

7. The brim of the black hat is then folded over a pre-made padded tube and pinned in place.
8. The brim is further shaped using an iron and the required edge marked.
9. Millinery wire is then sewn 1cm inside this line and the edge folded over the wire and stab-stitched into place.
10. A further fold is created on the opposite side and a band sewn in place.
11. The hat is lined. You can either make a lining to fit the crown or, as in this case, gather a length of fabric tightly and stick to the inside of the crown lightly, traditionally with a slight twist in the centre, then lightly sew around the lower edge and cover with a band of petersham. Be careful not to let the sewing show from the top side.

THE CLOCHE

12. After the initial fold, the felt is brought down and a further fold marked and created in the same way.
13. One side is brought down to fade out the folds and bring the felt into the nape of the neck.

14. Re-steam the hat continually until you get a smooth line around the neck.
15. Turn up the edge of the cloche and hold in place with tape.
16. Leave to dry thoroughly.
17. The edge can be further smoothed with an iron and more steam at this point.
18. Cut the edge to shape (in this case, some scalloped pinking shears were used for effect).
19. Decorate the cloche (in this case some tear-drop pieces of felt were cut and shaped and stab-stitched through the turned edge and some beads added).

Fig. 1.88 Add a pad to ensure a smooth curve over.

Fig. 1.89 Further iron and smooth, and mark the outer edge.

Fig. 1.90 Add the wire in the same way, fold over the edge and stab-stitch through.

Fig. 1.91 The pleat formed in the side and showing the lining in place.

Fig. 1.92 The finished hat by Marika Cholmondeley.

Fig. 1.93 Creating the first fold.

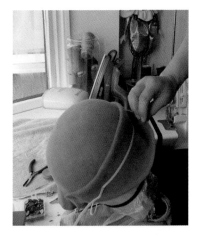

Fig. 1.94 Marking the second fold.

Fig. 1.95 Creating a folded wave.

Fig. 1.96 Pull the end of the folds down to smooth the back.

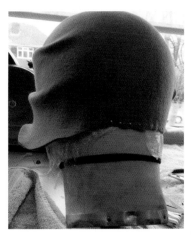

Fig. 1.97 Showing the back pulled in.

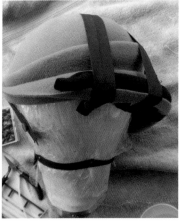

Fig. 1.98 Hold the brim up with spare tape.

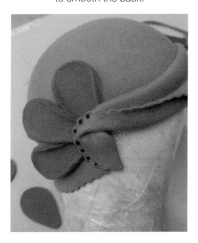

Fig. 1.99 Pink the edge and add decoration.

Fig. 1.100 The finished hat showing decoration.

Fig. 1.101 The finished hat showing the shape.

PROJECT 4 ART DECO HEADCOVERING

The art deco movement of the 1920s was a celebration of the exploration of many different influences and styles of the twentieth century, such as cubism, modernism and futurism.

The style contained influences from all over the world, especially Africa, Egypt and the Aztec forms and shapes. The Charleston and tango were the latest dance crazes, jazz was born and the singer Josephine Baker thrilled Paris.

The short hairstyles of the period were further emphasized with cloche hats and beaded headpieces. This pattern can be adapted to suit any colour, style or head size. Once you have mastered the basics, you can work out your own unique creations.

Materials Required

This example used the following materials:

- 3mm (1mm hole) clear glass beads with silver lining × 800
- 11mm teardrop black beads × 14
- 5.5mm diamanté cut set stones × 100
- 12mm drop clear stones × 5
- 10mm rectangle-cut, set stones × 5
- 4mm square black stones × 35
- 3mm black glass beads, 1mm hole × 600
- 3mm silver metal beads, 1mm hole × 600
- 2mm black beads × 1500 (for tassels)
- Strong waxed beading thread
- Long beading needle
- A head shape to the size required

Order of Work

1. Take a diamanté stone and pass a length of thread through the two holes on one side of the setting – add four clear stones – inside hole of a square diamanté – four clear – one black square – four clear – pass the thread through one side of the rectangle diamanté – four clear – the inside corner of the square – four clear – inside of second square diamanté – four clear – one black round. Continue up the other side as shown in Fig. 1.102.
2. Take the thread back through the centre and continue round the diamanté in the same fashion as described in (1), as shown in Fig. 1.103.
3. Your piece should look like Fig. 1.104.

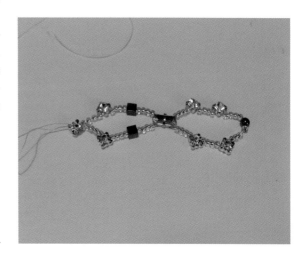

Fig. 1.102 The first leaf of the head plate completed.

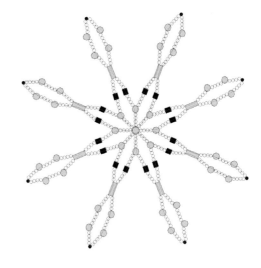

Fig. 1.103 Eight leaves joined together.

4. Fig. 1.105 shows the next row, and the direction of the thread. This row can also be seen in Fig 1.106. Six – one – six clear beads, square black bead, clear beads were used.

5. Fig. 1.107 shows the next row. Four – one – four, clear beads, round black bead, clear beads were used.

6. Figs 1.108 and 1.109 show the next step. These rows can be continued for as many rows as is necessary to cover the head to the top of the ears. In this example, four rows were completed.

7. Fig. 1.110 shows how a 'widow's peak' was achieved in the centre front.

8. Fig. 1.111 shows the next row, which provides the fringe row with slight shaping. The drawing shows the four columns at the back of the work. The sides are worked with six beads from the diamanté to the teardrop bead, as shown in Fig. 1.112.

9. Further shaping was achieved by working five rows of two × clear and two × black alternating beads in increasing rows. This is shown in Figs 1.113 and 1.115.

10. To further bring the beads down the sides, more rows were worked from each diamanté, as shown in Fig. 1.114. This completes the head piece.

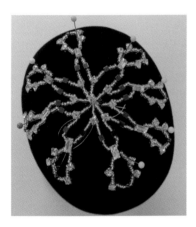

Fig. 1.104 Keep the piece on a head shape and hold in place with pins.

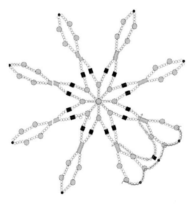

Fig. 1.105 Continue the work in orange and blue all the way round the piece.

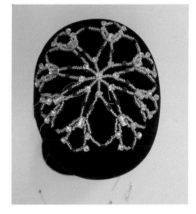

Fig. 1.106 Weave any loose threads through the beads to the outside of the piece.

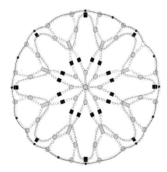

Fig. 1.107 The head plate finished.

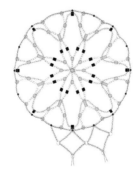

Fig. 1.108 The beginning of the sides of the piece.

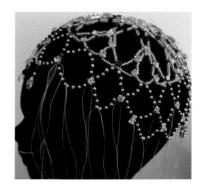

Fig. 1.109 The piece is beginning the take shape.

Fig. 1.110 Take the spare threads and shape the peak.

Fig. 1.111 Take this pattern from the side of the peak all round the piece. Add any more threads needed by threading more in, as shown in the diagram.

Fig. 1.112 The fringes give the piece character.

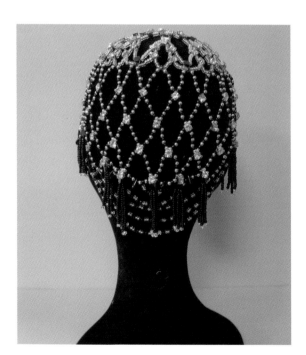

Fig. 1.113 The back beads are hanging free and can be adapted to any head size or hairstyle.

Fig. 1.114 More drapes to lengthen the sides. The finished piece.

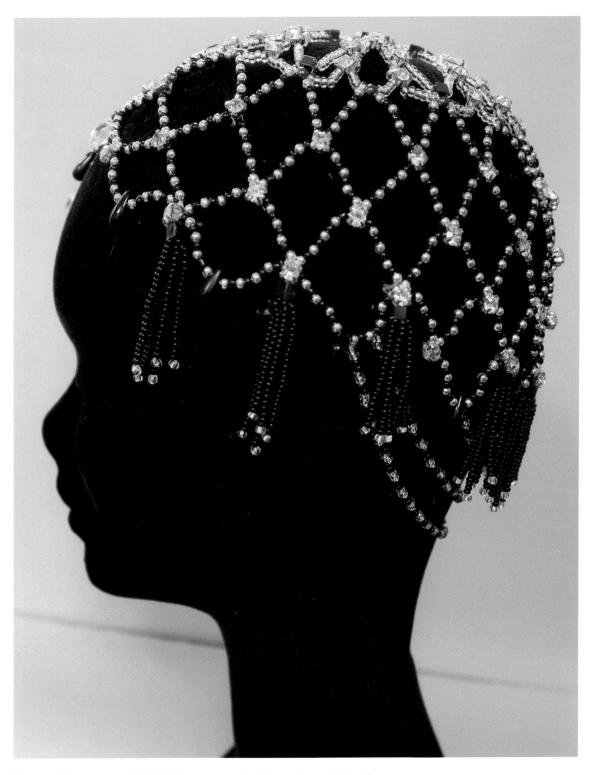

Fig. 1.115 The piece can be left like this or you could add more drapes to the side.

2
CROWNS

INTRODUCTION AND HISTORY

Throughout the periods and throughout Europe there have been an enormous variety and style of crowns. Derived from the Latin *corona*, meaning 'wreath' – the Greeks and Romans made crowns as honours from flowers, laurels, oak and, of course, later gold, and were awarded for athletic prowess, military valour (think Caesar) and on various other occasions.

We associate them most commonly with reigning Kings and Queens – an emblem of monarchy – but their use has always been far wider than that. Celtic Druids wore crowns, as do brides and grooms at their wedding in some cultures and religions (coronal or nuptial crowns) – indeed, a crown or corona was a wide form of recognition in olden times.

A crown could take a number of forms, from a pre-Columbian Native American headdress made of feathers from rare and beautiful birds, a diadem (a band) as worn by Persian Emperors and rulers of the later Roman Empire and a '*corona radiata*' – the radiant crown, also used by Roman Emperors, and as seen on the Statue of Liberty. Other variations include tiaras – which do not usually form a complete circle – and may be ornate in design. Royal tiaras were common among the Assyrian and Mesopotamian Kings. The oldest existing (intact) crown is the Iron Crown of Lombardy, which dates back to the fourth or fifth century AD. This crown is of a diadem type – a wide, ornamented gold band and enamel-work purportedly including a nail of the Cross.

The typical Royal Crown from the last thousand years in Europe has developed from the diadem band, and has had ornamentation progressively added to it. Commonly it has had crosses added over the band, representing the King's authority under Christ, and often the fleur-de-lys – associated with French royalty, and said to signify perfection, light and life. Arches were also fitted – front to back and side to side. Later, a *monde* was sometimes fitted. This was a sphere that represented the world that the monarch ruled. This, in turn, was topped with another symbol – often a cross in Christian countries.

In Britain, at present, we have three types of crown:

- Coronation: worn by monarchs when being crowned.
- State: worn by monarchs on other state occasions.
- Consort crowns: worn by a consort, signifying rank granted as a constitutional courtesy protocol.
-

Coronets are worn by nobility and others of high rank, and may vary in detail according to hierarchy, and are typically worn at state occasions.

It should be observed that it would be entirely impractical for a monarch to wear either a coronation crown or a state crown for everyday business, so the use of a circlet or diadem – or simply regalia – may often be used on stage. In the same vein, simpler crowns were fitted to helms and helmets for use with armour, providing clear identification of the Royal Personage.

As well as historical crowns, we also have a whole raft of such headgear to service film and television, in particular for the fantasy fiction genre – everything from *Narnia* to *Game of Thrones*. All require bespoke costumes and accessories – bringing more characterization into the subject than history allows. We have heroic characters and bad or even evil kings or queens to portray – providing scope for imaginative design and making.

PROJECT 1 A TAPERED CROWN

Crowns of the eleventh to thirteenth centuries in England tended to be of tapered form, i.e. the bands flared out as they rose, whereas the bands on later crowns were usually parallel. Portraits of the kings are a source of information and inspiration regarding this period, as the crowns themselves no longer exist.

Materials Required

- 1.4mm sheet brass at least 24 × 54cm
- Silver-solder
- Half-round beading for the edging
- Stone embellishments
- Strong glue

The first job is to decide how much the band should taper out (over what height), as this will dictate the radius of the circle from which the band material will be cut. A parallel band will, of course, all be straight lines, but as soon as it is tapered, it all becomes a curve, which needs to be defined.

Order of Work

1. Start by measuring the head of the actor, where the crown is likely to sit, and make allowance for any pad band if it is to be incorporated.
2. I then find it easiest to draw the band out to scale (or on computer with a CAD program) at the measured circumference/diameter (using pi to work it out – circumference = diameter × 3.142), ignoring the fact that heads aren't round for the moment, and then extend the tapering side lines (on the elevation drawing) to find the point of the cone they form. This line – cone point to bottom of band – becomes the inner radius of the circle from which the band is to be cut. We can then either work out mathematically how to cut the band to length, or cut it over-length and try it to see. In any event, it is strongly recommended to cut the band in paper (if necessary sellotape two pieces together) and work on the paper pattern before cutting any metal or leather.
3. Once you have cut this out and to length, you can join the two ends together, and you should find that the band should sit flat on a surface, with a nice, even taper to it, as anticipated. It should be fitted to the actor and any adjustments made, checking any allowance of an extra 0.5cm (say) for a leather band fitted internally for comfort.
4. The style of crown you make may be entirely plain, may have a profiled upper edge or may have detail such as fleur-de-lys added, and this should be factored in now, with the pattern altered or a new one made incorporating this detail. Ensure that the joint of the band is somewhere convenient – usually to the back, but if the band is profiled, the joint is best at the back on a narrow section, which may not be the exact rear. If it is possible to hide the joint behind a plaque or added detail, that would be ideal. Any additional detail, such as fleur-de-lys, should be carefully and accurately spaced out to avoid disappointment.
5. The tapered crown made in this example was made from brass, simply to show that it is not too complicated. It is not an exercise in a highly detailed replica – simply an exercise in a tapered, profiled band in metal, using (reasonably) basic tools.
6. The final paper template is printed out, or drawn by hand, and then glued to a piece of brass sheet using Pritt water-soluble (purple) for ease of cleaning off afterwards. The brass used in this example was 1.6mm thick, and was half-hard (brass is obtainable in different compositions, with different qualities – for a job like this it is not too critical what type is used). Being careful not to scratch the surface, a band saw with a metal-cutting blade was used to cut the shape out. It could be done carefully with hand saws, but a band saw

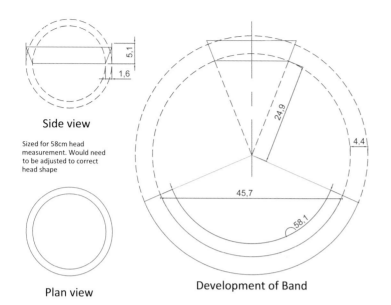

Side view

Sized for 58cm head measurement. Would need to be adjusted to correct head shape

Plan view

Development of Band

Tapered sides are extended to find the cone centre, and two circles are drawn from this centre point as shown. This will give the correct width and shape to create the taper. The length needed (in this instance 560mm of the inner circle) is calculated using Pi (3.14159).

The circumference of the inner circle will be 2r x Pi
(2 x 24.85cm = 49.7cm, x 3.14159 = 156.13cm

We require an arc length of 58cm. therefore:

360 / 156.13 (360 degrees devided by circumference of circle) = 2.384

2.384 x 58 = 133.73
(result multiplied by desired actual dimension = degrees of arc)

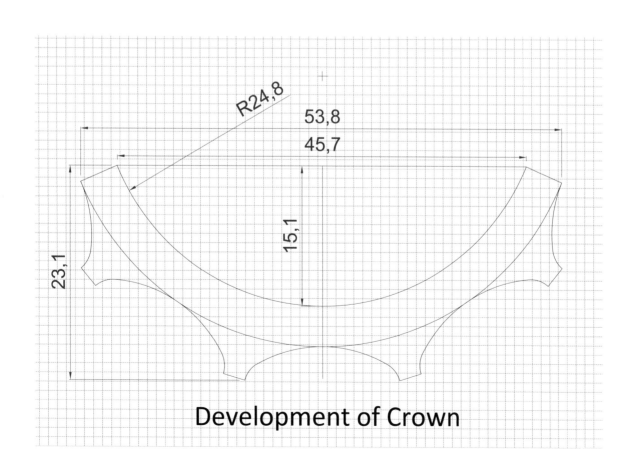

Development of Crown

is very much easier. If necessary, it would be possible to cut the band out of the brass sheet using a jigsaw with a metal-cutting blade fitted – but take care not to mark the surface. The cut edges were then cleaned up with a linisher (a bench-mounted belt-sander), the two processes being complete within 45min. The paper pattern was then stripped off and the brass cleaned and polished.

7. Bending material like this needs care so as not to kink it (which would then be very visible and hard to completely eradicate). Metals have a point of elasticity, where you can bend them and they will return. Further, and the bend becomes permanent. It is important to bend something like a crown band over a pipe or bar of a large diameter (about 75mm), so it will form a subtle bend. If you try bending it over a smaller bar – say 25–37mm – then the material will resist the first push and then suddenly 'give' and kink, rather than produce the gentle curve we want. (I used the supporting leg of a worktop to bend this to shape!) The technique is to produce a gentle bend, move it along 25mm, do it again and so on. It won't be nearly tight enough, so you repeat the process, as necessary, till you form the required head shape. As you go, you need to make the band slightly tighter than the top edge, so that the whole thing flares out as intended. Gentle bending and manipulation will be required to get the two ends to butt up together perfectly. The careful use of a soft hammer (with plastic faces) over a cobbler's last or even a pipe will help to line these up.

THE JOINT

8. There are several ways of joining the two ends together to make the 'circle'. One is to silver-solder as a butt joint (or weld if working in steel). Another would be to cut the band longer by 10–15mm and swage one end to form an overlap, and then to either silver-solder or rivet the joint and, finally, to 'plate' the joint,

i.e. solder or rivet a strip 20mm wide over the back of both halves of the joint.

9. This example has a very simple butt joint, silver-soldered. To hold it in position, I drilled four holes, 1mm diameter, two on each side of the joint, so I could stitch the joint together with twisted wire to ensure it didn't move during heating. I then mixed up some flux using borax powder and a little bit of water to make a thin paste, and brushed this on to and into my cleaned joint. I cut a couple of small pillions of silver-solder and laid them into the joint, and heated them with the blowtorch. In about 90sec the joint was up to temperature and flowing, whereupon I added a little more before finishing.

10. After cooling, the shape of the crown and the joint was gently adjusted into an oval shape using the soft hammer and last, and then the 'face' of the joint was carefully dressed on the linisher, so as to make it almost invisible. At this point, the crown could be fitted on the actor to get the exact shape.

11. Further polishing was then undertaken to remove all linisher marks using various grades of wet-and-dry, followed by Duraglit polish. This provides a crown of the fundamental tapered shape.

12. A little detail was added by silver-soldering half-round brass beading to the top edges of the crown, carefully bending them to shape first, and then clamping them in position for soldering with a blowtorch (the size a plumber would use), soldering about 75mm at a time, re-clamping and then soldering the next section along. When all pieces were soldered on satisfactorily, the crown was fully polished on a polishing mop.

13. A bag of large, cheap, plastic stones in gold-coloured mounts were bought online, and one was mounted with epoxy on the front face for simple decoration.

14. A parallel crown – as opposed to this tapered crown above – is somewhat simpler to draw out, and a parallel fleur-de-lys crown made in leather is also described next.

Fig. 2.1 The joint is silver-soldered, then rubbed down flat.

Fig. 2.2 After soldering, reshape the crown to the finished shape.

Fig. 2.3 Polish up the crown.

Fig. 2.4 D-shaped rod to be used for decorating the crown.

Fig. 2.5 Soldering the brass rod in place.

Fig. 2.6 The rod in place.

Fig. 2.7 Selecting the stone for decoration.

Fig. 2.8 Mixing milliput up to attach the stone.

Fig. 2.9 and Fig. 2.10 The finished crown.

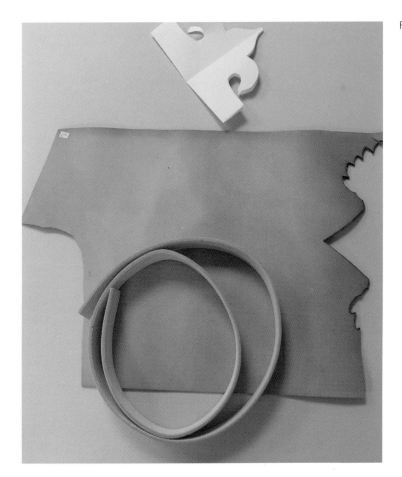

Fig. 2.11 The leather before we start.

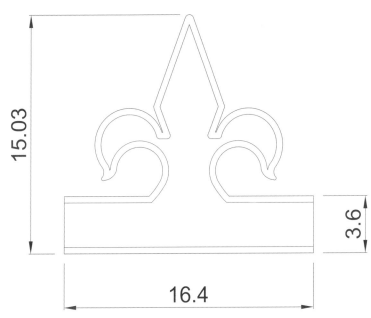

Fig. 2.12 The drawn-up pattern.

PROJECT 2 A LEATHER CROWN

Leather is a very satisfying material to use. It has substance and is malleable to a point. It can be tooled and shaped and planished into a shiny, round-edged piece. It can be dyed permanently and can even be worked to look like metal.

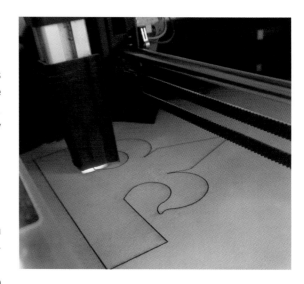

Fig. 2.13 The leather being lasered.

Materials Required

- 3mm thick, vegetable tan leather 50 × 50cm square, or buy an irregular shape that the pattern-pieces will fit
- 4mm × 70mm vegetable tan strip (enough to encircle the head, for this project 63cm)
- 16 screw rivets – 7mm shank
- Leather tools
  - ◦ A small skiver for shaping the edges
  - ◦ Small ball planisher
  - ◦ Edging smoother
  - ◦ Small circle punch for decoration
  - ◦ 4mm hole punch for riveting
- Black leather dye
- Black shoe polish
- A small amount of 0.2mm leather for decoration
- Cabochon stones for decoration
- Leather glue

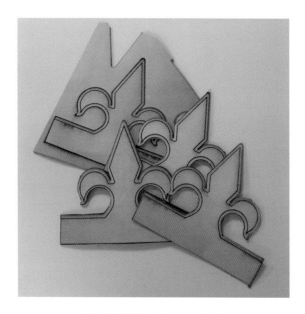

Fig. 2.14 All the pieces cut out.

Order of Work

1. The pattern for this crown is shown above. In this instance it was drawn up on AutoCAD and downloaded to a laser printer (see the section on Workshop Tools and Equipment in the Introduction for further information). This has the advantage of making smooth, precise edges, though it also deposits charcoal on the edges, which needs to be rubbed off. You could also draw it up manually and cut out with blades.
2. Now we need to work into the inner line and edge in order to round and smooth it off.
3. First, skive the edge with a skiving tool; this takes the sharp edge off (see Fig. 2.15). Then planish the edge with a planishing tool (you can get both manual and ones that will fit into a drill; these are, of course, faster to get the smooth finish you are require).
4. Now, work into the inner line, first to remove the build-up of charcoal, then to open it out slightly.

5. Place the pieces of shaped leather into a bowl of warm (not boiling) water until the bubbles that form cease.

> **TIP**
>
> If the water is boiling, you run the risk of 'cooking' the leather, which would result in shrinkage and hardening, which is difficult to get past.

6. Remove from the water and take the excess water off with a towel.
7. Find a former; this could be a large jar or, in this case, a large vase. Lay the pieces on to the former and leave to dry (Fig. 2.19). If you have no former, bend the pieces slightly between objects such as books (cover with cling film first to avoid wetting).

> **TIP**
>
> Leather glue, although it doesn't look like it, works better as a contact glue, i.e. spread a small amount on each surface and leave until touch dry, then place the leather together.

8. Take the leather band and cut to size, making sure the edges are perfectly straight and fit together well to form a band. Glue the edges together using leather glue.
9. Punch holes in each piece, as shown in Fig. 2.21, then offer these up to the band, mark and punch corresponding holes in the band.
10. Fit together using the screw rivets, to ensure a good fit.

> **NOTE**
>
> You can use normal or pop rivets; however, these screw rivets afford a certain amount of adaptability as the crown can be dismantled at any point. If using normal rivets, then leave the assembly of the crown till after dyeing.

11. Unrivet the crown and dye each piece on all sides, leave to dry – putting them back on the former to dry, to ensure that the pieces don't lose their shape with the dampness of the dye.
12. The dye might have left the leather a rather dull colour. You can use a leather polishing product or oil, or, as in this case, shoe polish, which, especially on black-dyed leather, does a good job of polishing and evening out the dye as you can see in Fig. 2.28.

> **TIP**
>
> Black shoe dye is also good for ageing any coloured dye and also gives it a richer look.

13. Reassemble the crown. You could stop here because you have the basic crown; however, you could also go on and decorate it. There are many things you could do: add more rivets, a velvet lining, add jewels or stones, anything that suits. Here, I have added a fur lining and tied it to the crown with leather thonging, using gold thread to keep it in place.
14. I also decided to add some stone cabochons. A good way of doing this is to make a leather setting. To do this you will need to make a former for the leather.
    a. Take a piece of 5mm plywood, at least three times the width of the stones.
    b. Draw round the cabochon.
    c. Cut the circle out with a piercing saw.
    d. Wet a small piece of 2mm leather.
    e. Place the cabochon on a backing piece of ply and lay the wet leather over the top. Put the former over the top so the leather-covered stone protrudes through the hole.
    f. Clamp together and leave to dry; this could be ready-dyed leather, or this could be done afterwards.
    g. Add any decorative tooling round the edge (this is better done when the leather is still slightly damp).
    h. Cut out and glue to the crown with the stone inside the setting.

Fig. 2.15 Skiving the edges.

Fig. 2.16 Rounding the edges by rubbing.

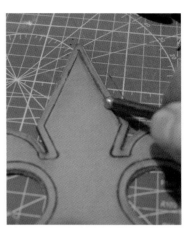

Fig. 2.17 Opening out the groove.

Fig. 2.18 Soaking the leather.

Fig. 2.19 Leaving to dry.

Fig. 2.20 The dried forms.

Fig. 2.21 The holes can be drilled or punched.

Fig. 2.22 The assembled crown.

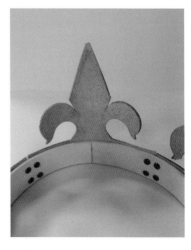

Fig. 2.23 From the inside.

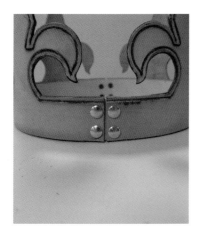

Fig. 2.24 The rivets form a decoration.

Fig. 2.25 Remember to dye the inside of the leather.

Fig. 2.26 The dyed pieces.

Fig. 2.27 Polish up with a leather polish.

Fig. 2.28 Showing the difference that polish makes.

Fig. 2.29 A crown is formed.

Fig. 2.30 With fur lining.

Fig. 2.31 Making a mould for the setting.

Fig. 2.32 Make sure there is room round the hole for the thickness of the leather.

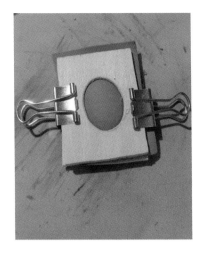

Fig. 2.33 Shape the leather using the mould and the cabochon.

Fig. 2.34 Stamp on any detail.

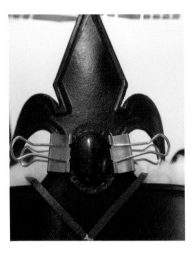

Fig. 2.35 Cut round the setting and stick to the crown using leather glue.

Fig. 2.36 The setting in place.

Fig. 2.37 The finished crown.

PROJECT 3 TIARA

Tiaras have been used to adorn the heads of the elite from the beginning of the human race (possibly before, as some animals also use adornments). Distinct from crowns, they are an open-worked piece of adornment, often made as an incomplete circlet and are usually associated with women. They can be made from any appropriate material, more than likely, originally, locally sourced, such as twigs, leaves and flowers. Then, being worked and manufactured using local and found materials, such as coral, carved wood and polished stones. Metals brought a new polished look to tiaras and cut stones finish the look of the present-day tiaras that we see on auspicious occasions.

If the tiara in this project was made from diamonds, set in silver or gold, the settings would be made appropriately and the whole project would be created using hard-soldering techniques. However, for this project I am using a very low-cost set of plastic stones and settings, and using soft solder and wire to set them in place. This means that none of the holes will be in a perfect place or necessarily match the other sizes. This is something we will have to overcome during manufacture.

Materials Required

- 0.3mm craft wire
- Stones with settings:
  - Horse eye shape 15mm × 52
  - Horse eye shape 12mm × 20
  - Horse eye shape 10mm × 34
  - Horse eye shape 8mm × 22
  - Teardrop shape 19mm × 1
  - Teardrop shape 14mm × 4
  - Octagon shape 6mm × 33
  - Octagon shape 4mm × 24
- Heat-adjustable soldering iron set at about 400°C
- Electrical grade soft solder (available at your local hardware store)
- Red flux (available alongside the solder)

- Fine-grade abrasive material, glass-fibre pen or fine-metal brush
- 0.36mm nickel silver sheet, 300 × 15mm
- Small dremel or hand drill
- Nose-shaped pliers

Fig. 2.38 Sorting the gems and shapes.

Fig. 2.39 Lay out the gems in the design you want.

Fig. 2.40 Cutting a strip for strengthening the band.

Fig. 2.41 A temperature-controlled soldering iron at approximately the correct temperature.

Testing the Techniques

It is important to test the technique you intend to use on a spare setting and piece of wire first. Cheap settings are made of metal but may have a heavy protective finish that can stop the solder from adhering. This can be helped in two ways: first, rubbing the inside of the setting with an abrasive (a glass-fibre pen or wire brush is useful for this) and also tinning the setting before starting the process.

TINNING

Tinning means coating the piece to be worked on with solder, making soldering to the surface much easier and more reliable. You can do this by putting a drop of the flux on the inside of the setting and placing a small amount of flux on top, then holding the heated soldering iron to the surface until the surface heats up sufficiently to melt the solder. It should pool across the surface. It may mean that no more solder is needed when it comes to the next process, though more can always be added.

Order of Work

1. Lay out your gems in the design required.
2. Starting with the upper sections of the pattern, take a piece of wire, generously long enough to loop the setting together in the shape required.
3. Make a flat loop at the end of the wire using your nose-shaped pliers, then take the wire through the setting holes (this will make the end of the wire adhere more strongly).
4. Pass the wire through the final setting and, again, make a loop for a strong connection. The wire can be bent, kinked or twisted in any way at this point in order to get the settings in the correct position. The solder will adhere better if the wire is touching the inside back of each setting.

Fig. 2.42 The final design decided.

Fig. 2.43 Small pieces of solder to be used; they can be picked up individually by the iron.

Fig. 2.44 Put the designed pieces together by threading wire through the settings.

Fig. 2.45 Add a drop of flux and a piece of solder in each setting.

Fig. 2.46 Hold the soldering iron on to the wire until the solder melts and sticks the wire in place.

Fig. 2.47 Get the next pieces ready.

WARNING

The fumes from the flux are toxic and may be injurious to health if inhaled, so work in a ventilated area to avoid this. The solder itself also includes flux and should be treated in the same way.

5. When the settings are sitting correctly, solder the wire into position, using the following method:
   - Place a drop of flux in each setting.
   - Place a small amount of solder in each setting (this may not be necessary if the piece has been tinned).
   - Heat the soldering iron to 400°C.

Fig. 2.48 Soldering the smaller pieces.

Fig. 2.49 All the top pieces ready
for the band.

Fig. 2.50 The setting placed in order.

Fig. 2.51 Putting the base
settings together.

Fig. 2.52 Wiring the top jewels in place.

Fig. 2.53 Cutting the metal strip to size.

- Hold the soldering iron on the wire/inside of the settings until the solder melts. You can manoeuvre the solder into position with the soldering iron until it sits over the wire.

6. Once you have created all the upper shapes, you can work on the band of the tiara.

7. Again, sit the settings in the position you want and put the top settings in position.

8. Take the wire, fold in half and put through the top and bottom of the settings at the same time (this stabilizes the settings better than taking the top and bottom of the settings separately).

NOTE

You will have to compensate for the different heights of the holes in the settings. Bend the wire between the settings until they all sit in the correct place. There is a bit of 'wiggle room' after the soldering to finalize the positions but the nearer you can get it at this stage, the better.

9. Wash your piece with soap or bathroom cleanser to erase any flux residue.

10. Make the final adjustments to the settings and carefully bend the tiara into shape.

> **NOTE**
>
> The easiest way to get a smooth curve on your band is to bend the tiara around a former or pull it around a wooden block.

11. Measure the inside of the band of the tiara once it has been bent into shape.

12. Cut a strip of the nickel silver, 10mm wide and as long as the inside band length (this measurement may vary slightly due to technique).

13. Rub this strip with a fine-grade abrasive paper and round the ends off for comfort.

14. For added practicality, drill five holes towards the bottom of the band in the centre and three holes at either end, to allow for the sewing-on of combs, should you need to do so.

15. To protect your soldering, no more heat should be applied to the piece; therefore, a strong, two-part epoxy resin adhesive is an ideal solution to stick the band to the back of the settings.

Fig. 2.54 The band in position.

Fig. 2.55 and Fig. 2.56 The finished tiara.

PROJECT 4 CHANCELLOR'S CHAIN

Plays such as *A Man for All Seasons* require unusual and distinctive regalia, which may need to be made. In this particular instance, Thomas More is adorned with his chain of office as Chancellor, which happens to be very distinctive, and is well known via a number of historical portraits.

Of course, there are many ways of making such a chain for stage use. One familiar way is to make a pattern of the distinctive 'S' link and take a latex mould from it.

Many years ago, I (as a DSM) made a pattern for the link from balsa, coated it in plastic padding before smoothing it down with wet-and-dry abrasive cloth to give is a good, polished surface. The pattern was placed on a smooth plate on which the latex mould could be made, and then latex was poured over it, and then poured off again. This left a thin layer of latex over the 'S' pattern, which was left to dry for about an hour until the white colour disappeared. More latex was poured over and poured off again to create another layer, and also left to dry until the white disappeared. This process was repeated, each one partially drying before the next one was applied, until six or so layers of latex had been applied, giving a total thickness of 1–3mm. When enough layers had been built up, it was left to vulcanize to a light amber colour.

When dry, the mould should be thoroughly dusted with talcum powder, otherwise it will instantly stick to itself and only come apart with damage. The pattern can now be carefully removed from the latex mould, and the inside again thoroughly dusted and cleaned off with talc. The mould is now ready for use.

If using brushes with latex, they should be rinsed in a solution of soap and water, before and after use, to aid cleaning and to prolong their life. If a thinner viscosity is needed for the first coat of latex, to pick up more detail, the brush latex may be diluted with a small amount of distilled water.

Fig. 2.57 and Fig. 2.58 The finished chain.

All those years ago, the chain links were cast in the latex moulds using casting resin and either painted gold – or maybe had gold filler added. Certainly gold powders are widely available as resin fillers.

Each link was mounted to a brass link chain to form the regalia.

The technique of casting certainly still holds good – indeed we have a wider array of materials available to us – even white-metal or pewter casting (not new) followed by electro-plating.

3D printing has provided us with another viable method for making props such as these. Because the 'S' links are practical, it was decided to use FDM filament printing to make the components, so that they would be strong enough to work as a chain without breaking.

Making the Chain Using a 3D Printer

MATERIALS REQUIRED

- A 3D printer (see the section on Workshop Tools and Equipment in the Introduction for further information).
- 3D filament 1.25mm
- Milliput two-part putty
- Gold-paint spray
- Brass-link chain
- Pliers

ORDER OF WORK

1. The 'S' was drawn in DesignSpark Mechanical (use any 3D drawing program that will export an STL file or similar) with four link rings – one on each corner, using period paintings for reference – and the result imported into FlashPrint, which is the slicing program for the Flashforge Finder.
2. Within FlashPrint, the 'S' model can be resized as desired – in practice, the letters are 35mm high – and the quality of print can be set. These were printed at 'fine', not 'hyper', which is best quality. These settings are a balance of time against finish and given FDM printing will never give you a perfect finish, 'hyper' is rarely used.
3. Twenty 'S' links were printed, taking about 20min each. The surface of these showed the filament grain as was expected. A blob of Milliput epoxy putty was mixed up, and a small amount worked into the surface of each link just to smooth it out. The links were then sprayed with grey primer prior to final finish.
4. Trials were done with finishing. Imitation gold-leaf was not very successful, as it was a little coarse for what is, in effect, jewellery. Lacquer-based gold finish did not give the desired effect either, and it turned out that the most successful was a gold aerosol paint.
5. A pair of portcullises were then drawn and printed in exactly the same way, painted and put aside for assembly.

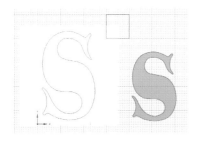

Fig. 2.59 The 'S'-shape drawn.

Fig. 2.60 The 'S'-shape drawn in 3D.

Fig. 2.61 The practice print.

Fig. 2.62 The 'S' smoothed over with milliput. 3D prints can be smoothed by melting with acrylic or rubbing down, but this method proved very successful.

Fig. 2.63 The Tudor rose, printed.

Fig. 2.64 All the components ready for milliput.

Fig. 2.65 Smoothed over and painted.

Fig. 2.66 The assembly begins.

Fig. 2.67 The rose in gold.

6. The final part was the gold Tudor rose. Most people's 3D drawing/sculpting would not be this advanced – and mine certainly is not! Fortunately, there are so many 3D designs available to download on the internet that one was found with little difficulty, and resized on the FlashPrint program and printed out very successfully. This again was primed and painted gold.

7. Brass open-link chain was bought from Amazon, and the various 'S' links, portcullis and rose were assembled using individual brass chain links with pliers, to build up to the Chancellor's chain.

Making the Chain with Pewter

MATERIALS REQUIRED

- A small amount of 2mm MDF
- Lead-free pewter no. 2
- Clamps to hold the mould
- Pewter melting-pot

As a practical example of a stylized pewter casting alternative, a mould was made from layers of 2mm MDF – in this instance, laser-cut for convenience. The photographs illustrate the internal form of the mould, with the large 'V' at the top providing the gate in which the molten pewter is poured, and also showing the small ventilation passages that line up with the bottom rings. These vents allow trapped air to escape and be displaced by the pewter in order to achieve a good fill and ensure that the rings cast cleanly. Without adequate vents, trapped air can prevent the metal from reaching all details.

The pewter used was lead-free pewter no. 2 from Tiranti's. This has a melting point of 220°C and a suggested operating temperature of 265–280°C. Because we only do very occasional casting, we have a very basic and cheap melting-pot (which has been perfectly adequate for our needs), costing around £30. The pot has a capacity of more than 1kg of pewter, which we shall never exceed.

The MDF plates of the mould were clamped together by a number of clamps – remembering that it will get much heavier when it has molten metal poured into it! The work area was made safe, and the assembled mould, together with the melting-pot, were placed together on a large, steel, baking tray to contain any spillages and to make a safe fireproof work surface. The pot was turned on and the pewter heated, and a little flux powder added, which helps flow and separates out any impurities. When the pewter was fully up to temperature, the dross (impurities) floating at the top was scraped off and removed with a spoon to leave clean, bright molten metal. The ladle was placed in the metal for half a minute to warm up as well.

The ladle was then filled and, while steadying the large clamp holding the mould (if in doubt, wear leather gauntlets), the full ladle was moved across to the mould and poured in the top gate.

The ladle was then put to one side and the mould left to cool for 5min. After this, the mould clamps were removed and we could see that the casting was perfect. It was removed from the mould, sprues cut off and returned to the melting-pot, which was then turned off and allowed to cool naturally.

Pewter can be cleaned up with fine files (carefully) but use chalk on the face of the file to help prevent pinning. Wet-and-dry is absolutely fine to use, and also machine polish with care.

We have shown layered MDF moulds, but pewter may also be cast in moulds made from RTV-101 high-temperature silicone rubber, which is extremely useful for making items of more irregular shape.

Fig. 2.68 Three parts of the MDF mould; there are six altogether, including end plates.

Fig. 2.69 The melting-pot.

Fig. 2.70 Hold the mould pieces together with clamps.

Fig. 2.71 The pewter melting.

Fig. 2.72 Mix and remove impurities.

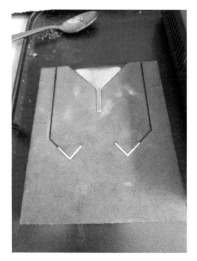

Fig. 2.73 After pouring with the back removed.

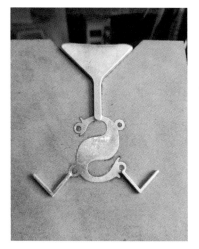

Fig. 2.74 Showing the back of the 'S'.

Fig. 2.75 Showing the front of the 'S'.

Fig. 2.76 The 'S' cleaned up.

Fig. 2.77 The finished 'S'.

3
CANES, STICKS AND STAFFS

INTRODUCTION AND HISTORY

The words canes and sticks are interchangeable through modern history, though it is likely that canes originated from China and were made of cane. In modern times, the cane tends to mean a stick without a hook on the top. Staffs were longer – at least to the shoulder.

The assumption is that there have been sticks and staffs as long as humans have existed. Gorillas have been seen to use sticks as a walking aide, so it might have been even earlier. They have been used to aid walking and as an extension of the arm as a weapon and tool. The stick/staff also developed as a means of identification, fashion, wealth, power, faith and later, as a smuggling device.

The earliest recorded manufactured stick was in Ancient Egypt around 4000BC. During the seventeen to the nineteenth centuries, a person of means was not deemed properly attired without a cane.

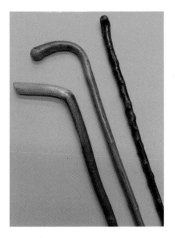

Fig. 3.1 A selection of early sticks (*from left*): the handle taken from the shape of a tree; an early bentwood handle; an example of a blackthorn stick.

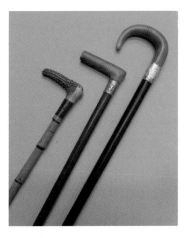

Fig. 3.2 A selection of handles made from antlers and horn.

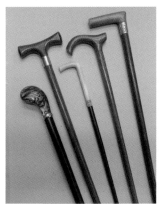

Fig. 3.3 A selection of different types of handles (*from left*): a pistol grip; a T-handle; a ladies' L-handle; an opera handle; an L-handle; all popular in the nineteenth/ twentieth centuries.

Fig. 3.4 A selection of gadget canes (*from left*): a sword stick; a telescope stick; a shooting stick (creating a stool).

Parts of a Cane

Handle This can be in the form of a knob or a handle, with the main shapes being L, crutch, opera, crook and pistol, some of which are shown in Fig. 3.3.

Collar This is a ring of metal, invented to disguise the join of the handle to the shaft, but also used as a decoration, to increase the value of the stick and to hold the identification of the owner.

Shaft This is the length of material (usually wood) that defines the height of the stick. Other materials that have been used are cane, bamboo, rattan, glass, bone, metal and plastic.

Eyelet This is a hole that is sometimes present towards the top of the stick, which allows for a wrist loop or decoration.

Ferrule This is a metal ring attached tightly to the bottom of the shaft to protect the wood from splitting. It is also the name given to the rubber protective end, which also prevents slippage.

Medieval and Before

Although it is without doubt that walking sticks have always existed for practical reasons, as both a walking aid and a fighting stick, they have also always been symbols and indicators of power by all the ancients. The best sticks would be given to the most deserving or the most powerful and would be decorated with locally sourced paints, dyes, beads or feathers.

Merchants would have their own personalized sticks, as well as many other professions, including shepherds, who would use a crook to rescue lambs, as well as to fend off attackers. The shepherd's crook was taken by the Catholic Church as a symbol of gathering the flock and turned in to extremely ornate croziers. European kings also used the cane, for showing power and wealth, and they were given as gifts.

An early stick was the blackthorn, which was a stick made from the blackthorn tree. It originated in Ireland where it was also named the shillelagh. An example of this is on the right in Fig. 3.1. The blackthorn often had a round knot at the end, taken from a natural knot in the tree. The shillelagh was well known for use in fighting.

Fifteenth to Eighteenth Centuries

Many of the European walking sticks were carved during this time and individually made for the owner. These canes were called 'folk art', a term still in use today for a handmade stick.

In 1600, sticks/canes became part of everyday dress and increasingly were used as an ornament. Very few had collars; if they did, then they were silver, occasionally gold or brass.

During the eighteenth century, the ferrules were also made of brass, were between 150 and 200mm long and had an iron pad protruding from the end. This was to cope with the deep mud and effluent-covered ground they had to walk through.

Seventeenth to Nineteenth Centuries

As men stopped wearing swords, they began to 'wear' canes. Until the late seventeenth century, the stick was usually made in one piece, though if there were separate handles, they were of Malacca with knobs of ivory or bone, sometimes metal or porcelain. You also sometimes saw T-shaped sticks – they didn't usually have a collar. By 1700, canes were dandified with handles or knobs, becoming richly ornate. Gold was used, as well as rare stones and carvings. There were also staffs with ribbons and bows for the fops to show off. Towards the end of the eighteenth century, you were required to obtain a licence to hold a walking stick and adhere to the 'rules' of etiquette that were established.

From the middle of the nineteenth century, antlers and horns were popular handles and the join was covered by a wide, plain collar and ferrule of nickel, silver plate or plain iron, as shown in Fig. 3.2. The stick on the left is the handle of a riding crop. In the 1850s, we see ferrules often 5cm long. During the Victorian Industrial Revolution, Europe had the newly rich middle class who fuelled the rise of ornate and precious walking sticks that were so much a part of their dress. The sticks began to be mass-produced, which meant that the highly decorated sticks became available to more people. Handmade sticks became prized possessions, with animal and bird heads as handles very popular, as well as porcelain handles, painted or enamelled with everything from flowers to naked ladies in repose.

In the 1850s, it was popular to have collars with embossed dots around the edges. The ferrules were shorter during this period, often only 2.5cm long. In the 1850s, we first see the wooden sticks curved into a crook for a handle. They were first made with a gentle curve, but quickly lengthened into the shape of today.

In the second-half of the nineteenth century and into the twentieth, sticks continued to be popular. The collars were brass-plated silver, then nickel and chrome, with a small ferrule of iron or steel – usually about 12mm.

In 1898, a form of self-defence was developed from Japanese techniques such as Kodokan Judo by Edward William Barton-Wright; this, he called Bartitsu, which is immortalized in the fight between Holmes and Moriarty in the Sherlock Holmes' novels. The technique was widely taught and contests took place between the gentry.

Twentieth to Twenty-First Centuries

The art deco period of the 1920s saw a resurgence in fashion canes and many of the most ornate were made in these times.

After 1920, through the twentieth century, the stick became much less used as a weapon or for fashion, but more as a walking aide. In 1931, Guilly d'Heremont in France created a white cane for the visually impaired, and this quickly spread throughout the world. Starting as a painted stick, it developed into a foldable metal stick, and again further with a ball on the end for ease of feeling the ground and objects around.

Some gadget sticks, such as the hunting stick shown in Fig. 3.4, have been developed to include camping chairs. Other sticks include the riding crop, often with an antler handle, which has become less ornate. Traditional ceremonial sticks, such as the 'Black Rod', are seen in the opening of the British Parliament, and the ornate croziers of the Catholic Church and the yard sticks of the military.

PROJECT 1 CANE MADE WITH DOOR KNOB

Making canes can be a lengthy process. Here we show how easy it is to make an authentic-looking eighteenth-century-style cane using readily available materials. One of the things that makes a Victorian cane look good is to make the shaft taper towards the ferrule. This can, of course, be turned on a lathe or worked with a rasp and abrasive papers. However, in this case, the shaft of a long snooker cue served very well. The best cue to get is that of a handle of a bridge cue, which is long enough to cut without needing to include the screw join that cues have. When cut to length, the cue also has the perfect dimensions that allow for the commonly sold copper tubing of 15 and 22mm to fit perfectly as a collar or a ferrule.

The knob can be made from many different door knobs, some of which are shown in Fig. 3.5. The door knob also has a threaded connection that lends itself very well to attaching to the shaft.

Fig. 3.5 The door-knob cane is an example of a porcelain cane, popular in the eighteenth century.

Fig. 3.6 A selection of door knobs appropriate for canes tops.

Materials Required

- A snooker cue, allowing a straight shaft of 112mm
- A small piece of 15mm copper tubing
- A small piece of 22mm copper tubing
- A small piece of rubber
- A door knob with a base that will sit well on top of the 22mm copper tubing
- A strong adhesive, such as DevCon epoxy
- Masking tape, fret saw, hack saw and 15mm hole punch
- A wood file and drill

Order of Work

1. Discard the thicker part of the cue (this could be used later to make a staff).
2. Mark a length of 112mm, taking a little off each end of the cue. (The actual length is shown in Figs 3.7 and Fig. 3.8.)
3. Wind some masking tape around the shaft and cut with the fret saw, as shown in Figs 3.9 and 3.10.
4. Cut 40mm of the 22mm copper tubing and 30mm of the 15mm copper tubing.
5. Cut a section of rubber with the hole punch (Figs 3.14, 3.15 and 3.16).

6. Mark a point 25mm from the end of the narrower end of the shaft and, using a wooden file, smoothly file away the wood until the copper tube fits snugly.
7. This should leave a small area that the rubber stop will fit into to allow for a rubber ferrule. Stick this in place (Figs 3.18 and 3.19).
8. Do the same on the top end. Try and make the cut edge as straight and clean as possible, as this is going to show on the finished cane.
9. Before you put the collar on, drill a hole straight into the top of the shaft, large enough for the screw of the door knob to fit snugly.
10. Glue the three pieces together using the epoxy glue.

Fig. 3.7 Select your cane and measure the required length.

Fig. 3.8 Take into account the width of the cane and cut the length appropriately.

Fig. 3.9 Cover the area to be sawn with masking tape to ensure a clean cut.

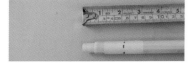

Fig. 3.10 Showing the thin end. Cut where it is 15mm in diameter.

Fig. 3.11 The top (thick) end. Using a jig will ensure an even cut.

Fig. 3.12 This will be the bottom, and now needs the diameter reducing to fit the 15mm diameter copper tube.

Fig. 3.13 The end should have a diameter of 15mm; select the equivalent copper tube.

Fig. 3.14 The rubber used here is from a flipflop shoe.

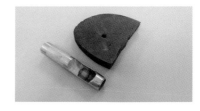

Fig. 3.15 Using a leather/wood hole punch.

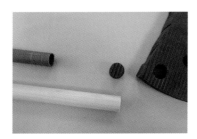

Fig. 3.16 The rubber will expand slightly, which will help a good, push-in fit.

Fig. 3.17 Offer the rubber on to the end of the stick.

Fig. 3.18 From this picture, the stick is filed down slightly to allow the stick to push inside the tube ferrule, as shown in Fig. 3.21, which shows the top end.

Fig. 3.19 Glue the ferrule and
rubber in place to complete the bottom end.

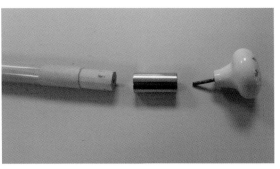

Fig. 3.21 Showing the filed top, drilled. The knob screw has
been cut slightly shorter and the pieces offered together to
ensure a good fit.

Fig. 3.22 Glue the pieces together using strong,
two-part epoxy resin.

Fig. 3.20 Tighten the knob screw in place.

PROJECT 2 CANE WITH PRINTED HANDLE

For quite a few years, FDM printers were the only affordable 3D printers available. Compared to SLA (stereolithography) printers, they are rather crude, although faster. However, for printing something like a prop cane handle, they are extremely good, as PLA filament is strong and robust, and, therefore, not easily damaged. PLA filament is also available in a remarkable range of colours and even materials – although some colours, such as gold and silver, are perhaps a little optimistic. An FDM printer works rather like a very fine and accurate glue-gun – depositing a fine string of molten plastic from a heated nozzle on a moving printer head, on to a work table that drops down a fraction after every 'slice' has been drawn by the nozzle.

Materials Required

- 3D printer (see the section on Workshop Tools and Equipment in the Introduction for further information)
- 3D printing filament
- A donor stick
- Windsor and Newton water-soluble oil paint – raw umber
- Devcon epoxy glue or equivalent
- Copper tube – a small amount of 22mm and 19mm

Order of Work

1. For this cane, a stylized wolf's head was chosen from a website called Thingiverse.com. Many or most of the designs/downloads are free to use on a non-commercial basis, and files can be downloaded in STL format. 3D printers usually come with 'slicing' software, which allows you to reduce or enlarge the STL object, rotate it, add rafts and supports (to ensure that all bits print), and then calculate the thousands of layers necessary to build it – slice by slice.

2. The output file from the 'slicer' can then be transferred to the printer, which will then get on with it. We chose to use our Flashforge Finder FDM printer – now quite an old machine, but still extremely good – and to print a trial in 'gold' filament. This printed well, but disappointed as a colour. Moreover, the handle was just a little small in the hand. For the actual object, we chose to print it in 'ivory' PLA, and it was enlarged to 115 per cent of its original size, using the scale facility. There are also

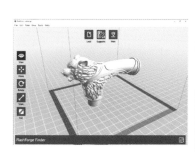

3.23 The pattern, downloaded from the website.

3.24 The start of the printing process.

3.25 The handle with supports in place.

3.26 The handle with the supports removed in brown-coloured filament.

3.27 The handle resized, in gold filament.

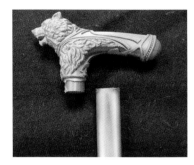

3.28 Filed slightly to fit the tube collar.

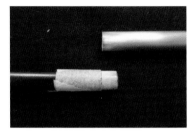

3.29 Filing the cane top to fit the tube collar.

3.30 The finished resized cane top.

3.31 Comparing the colours.

four different quality settings: low, standard, fine, and hyper. If you are printing a bracket where aesthetics don't matter, use the low or standard setting. Use hyper when trying to get as much detail as possible from the machine, but it does make the process much longer. This handle was printed in 'fine' and still took nearly 18hrs to print!

3. Since this printed overnight, it was good to see that it printed well. It was removed from the printing table and all the supports cut off. Very little other trimming or cleaning was needed, though some very fine dressing to the grip was done with a small, flat, needle file to ensure it was as smooth as possible on the hand.

4. The cane itself was bought already tapered and pre-painted black, and simply needed the handle fitting and a ferrule fitting to the bottom. The handle, as printed, has a spigot that (when printed to 115 per cent) was the perfect size to sleeve into 22mm copper (plumbing) pipe,

obtainable from any large DIY outlet. A 35mm length of this was used, cut off using a normal plumber's pipe-cutter (small). The top of the wooden cane was marked all around about 19mm down, keeping it square by wrapping masking tape round it and lining the top of the tape up. A knife was used to score a ring in the wood at this height and a file used to gently reduce the diameter (to the scribed ring) to push-fit the copper tube.

5. Before actually fitting the handle, the ivory was 'aged' using Windsor and Newton water-soluble oil paint (raw umber), applied in the corners using a very fine brush and then run along the corners using a drop of thinner. Any excess was wiped off with a kitchen towel.

6. The copper pipe was treated to a rub-down with silver-plating solution, and then buffed up. The ferrule for the bottom was simply a 15mm length of 18mm-diameter brass tube from stock, which is available from model suppliers

such as Squires or Eileen's Emporium. Again this was cut using a tube cutter, and this was hammered on to the end.

7. The handle, tube and cane assembly was checked to make sure it all fitted together nicely, then a little Devcon epoxy glue mixed and applied to half the inside of the tube, and the tube fitted to the cane – making sure that there wasn't too much glue in the bottom of the hole to get in the way of the handle when that was inserted. Once dry, more glue was mixed and applied inside the tube, and the handle pushed in. If necessary, carve a groove in the handle spigot to allow the air to escape. Ensure the handle is fully home and square when drying.

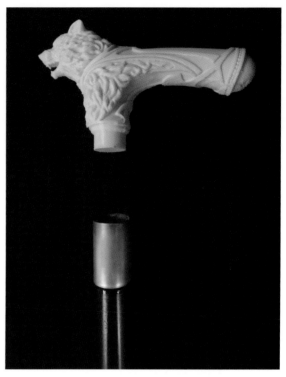

3.33 Glue the handle in place.

3.32 Showing the handle after colouring.

3.34 The finished cane.

4
GLOVES

INTRODUCTION AND HISTORY

Gloves have been around for thousands of years, the earliest possibly being mittens made for protection against the cold, either sewn with animal skin or knitted with wool. Very soon, they were used as a sign of wealth. Gloves were found in the tomb of Tutankhamun, which would have dated them to 1323BC; these were linen, and finely decorated.

Gloves have been both practical and used as an accessory to clothes throughout time to the present day and have been used in many different situations. They have been decorated with the

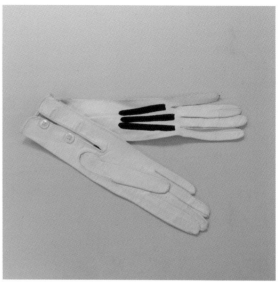

Fig. 4.2 Kid gloves of the Victorian era.

symbols of someone's faith, they have been worn to match a person's clothes or to protect a person from the weather, and used as tools of work such as welding and blacksmithing, as well as to protect others from the wearer in the case of surgeons.

Medieval and Before

Gloves didn't always have fingers or thumbs but originally resembled baby's mittens. Women wore them to protect their hands. The thumb was the first part to evolve, with the fingers coming quickly afterwards – though mittens were, and still are, preferred to give maximum protection from the cold.

Gloves were generally used by men and created for protection, made from fabric/skins that were available at the time and in the local area.

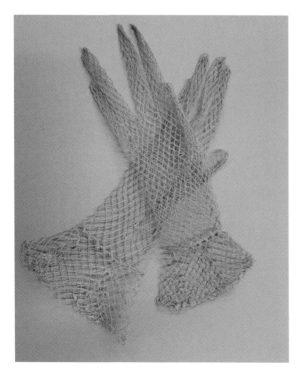

Fig. 4.1 Knotted gloves, c.1910.

The main things that men needed protection from were fighting and the elements, though there is evidence that the Vikings brought gloves of wool and flax. At this point they sometimes had a foldable cuff.

The gauntlet was originally an armoured glove, made from leather or strong fabric with metal articulating 'scales' or 'plates' riveted on. The glove would cover the wrist for further protection and would be made bespoke for the individual fighter. Only the richest would be able to afford to have a fully armoured gauntlet. A less expensive option would be made from strong leather and would be quite loosely fitted, maybe with chain-mail protection. The gauntlet was intended to deflect sword and arrow blows (especially while holding a shield, when the hand was particularly vulnerable). However, it also had the effect of intimidation and, of course, could inflict greater damage from a backhand blow to the enemy. The armoured gauntlet would have been made from forged iron and later steel. Certainly around the sixteenth century, they were used to show status and were embellished with gold and silver.

It wasn't until the fifteenth century that gloves started to become a fashion item, and even then, used more to show status rather than following any fashion trend as we know it. Gauntlets might be worn out of battle if they were particularly well made and this led to them being made for the rich without the intention to be used in battle.

Sixteenth Century

Gloves played a part in many religious ceremonies, not least in the Christian Mass when gloves would be donned, to be removed at certain points to signify the purification of the hands, as Jacob had in the bible, and removed again for intimate moments, such as consecrating the wine. Ecclesiastical gloves became delicately decorated with beautiful gold- and silver-work. They were made of linen rather than leather and were, and are, highly revered by the church.

Fabric gloves were generally becoming more popular. Soft and malleable fabrics were used, fuelled by the importation of cotton, and the growing number of cotton-producing mills in Britain made the gloves more affordable to more people.

The gloves were mostly still gauntlets in the sixteenth century and were highly decorated with gold- and silver-work, metal lace and intricate embroidery on the skirt, while the main part of the glove remained plain.

Metal gauntlets were still widely used and would be made from material as good as the wearer could afford. Steel was becoming available and, being significantly lighter than chainmaille, was prized by the elite.

Seventeenth Century

Knitted gloves were becoming popular and they were often made from cotton, though leather and woven fabric gloves were still widely worn.

There was a huge divide between gloves that were worn for practical purposes and the ones that were prized possessions, which might be bought as gifts and rarely worn, maybe only to be held in a portrait painting.

The highly decorated gauntlet gloves of the previous century were still popular, the skirt of the glove often being made from a different material from the hand section. This was probably because the decoration would have been carried out as a separate job from the actual glove-making and attached at the end of the process. It afforded the opportunity to reassign it at the end of the life of the glove. Early in the century, the gauntlet skirt was often cut into sections or 'tabs', though this was less fashionable after 1830.

The gauntlet skirts were often embroidered with gold-work and carried a family crest, animal scenes or beautiful images, captured in plaques and edged in gold or silver lace. Through the century, more delicate silk embroidery became popular; beadwork was also seen.

The fingers were often extended in the more elaborate gloves – possibly as long fingers were seen to be beautiful at the time or just showing that the wearer need not have practical gloves.

The range of practical gloves was extensive, and worn when partaking in sport or work. Gentlemen would wear fitted gloves for riding or hunting and any worker would protect their hands, if they could, with gloves.

Gloves became part of the outfit and in the second half of the century, men's gloves became shorter and ladies' were more in keeping with their dresses. The new fashions had sleeves just below the elbow and often the gloves would be long enough to meet them.

Eighteenth Century

There were many inventions aiding the manufacture of gloves in the eighteenth century, which meant finer leather was available and more people were wearing them as part of their outfit.

Men wore gloves less frequently for formal occasions, and by the middle of the century, it became unfashionable for a man to wear highly decorated gloves with gauntlet skirts, though gauntlet gloves were worn for protection while working, riding or when it was cold. If extra protection was needed, such as for a furrier or blacksmith, the gauntlets were made from heavier leather. Everyday gloves were short and mostly made of fine leather.

Chamois leather became popular as a material for gloves; this was made from a mountain goat (later sheep) and because it was oil-tanned, it was washable, which had huge benefits, of course.

In polite society, it was fashionable for ladies to cover much of the skin, to keep it untanned, showing that they didn't have to work, and also to cover up any skin conditions. Young ladies were also encouraged to wear gloves when greeting anyone, for cleanliness. These were fairly plain but were often embellished with embroidery of plants and flowers. The fine leathers and knitted fabrics allowed for longer gloves and many portraits show women wearing gloves up to the elbows.

Fine mittens and fingerless gloves were also popular. Knitted, crocheted or knotted cotton gloves could be worn throughout the day, and the mittens, although less practical, allowed for uninterrupted embroidery on the back of the hand; they were often made from silk, with fine leather palms.

MOURNING GLOVES

It was encouraged to have specially trimmed gloves for mourning and for attending funerals. This could mean wearing black gloves or having some existing gloves, trimmed in black. The gloves would be plain in nature.

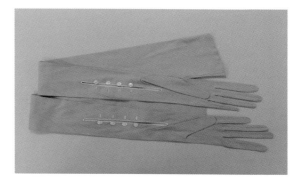

Fig. 4.3 Long-length kid gloves.

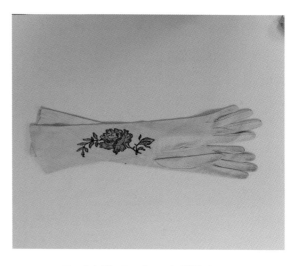

Fig. 4.4 Shorter, decorated kid gloves.

Nineteenth Century

Gloves became more sombre for men and women during the last part of the nineteenth century. However, more inventions in the manufacture of gloves, many in France, meant that more gloves were available to everyone, and they were more fitted.

The 1830s saw uniform sizing, which was taken up by an Italian manufacturer and gained recognition around the world, although bespoke glove-making was still very much the norm.

Mourning gloves were still expected. While the men's gloves remained sombre, the ladies became increasingly 'pretty' and delicate features often became incorporated into the design.

There was the etiquette in polite society of always wearing gloves when greeting, or touching hands, this for men and women. Also, gloves were expected to be worn in church and all formal occasions, except when eating. Servants were also expected to wear gloves for cleanliness.

Gloves were often made of fine leather, though also of cotton or silk. Fine silk jersey was available, enabling close-fitting, arm-length gloves. It really depended on the length of the sleeve that was in fashion at the time as to how long the glove was. When in short-sleeved evening wear, ladies might be wearing longer gloves, though they did not venture over the elbows until towards the end of the century. Generally speaking, the length of the daywear sleeves for men and women were longer, therefore, the gloves were short, except when the activity demanded more protection, i.e. riding or working as a furrier/blacksmith or, in the case of servants, cleaning shoes or silver – in this case sleeve protectors were usually worn. These consisted of a tube of cotton, fastened top and bottom, to cover the sleeves to prevent them from getting dirty.

The second half of the century saw, increasingly, decorated gloves for women, many being finely embroidered on the back of the hand. You saw an elasticated wrist, or elastic woven into the fabric to ensure a closer fit. Many European countries being

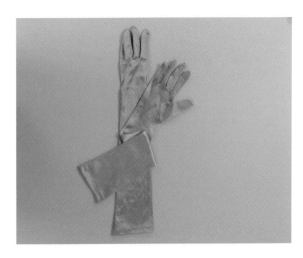

Fig. 4.5 Long, evening, satin jersey gloves.

ahead of us in manufacture imported cheaper and in the case of France, finer gloves. Men's gloves became more colourful, with specific designs for the activity they were pursuing.

Netted or open knitted gloves were very popular in the second half of the century, often worn by ladies as a fashion item, and because they were more easily made at home, they were available to everyone with a little time to spend on the craft.

Twentieth Century

Although for much of the century gloves were an essential part of dress, and although there were pockets of high-fashion-related, glamorous gloves, for the most part, gloves remained rather plain throughout the 1900s.

Men would wear darker-coloured gloves during the day and paler in the evening. The style would be short with three rows of pointing on the outer side, with a button on the inside of the wrist – a style still seen today in formal wear.

The First World War brought shortages in leather for such things, so knitted gloves became popular and there was also a move to practical gloves, such as mittens, to protect again the weather, rather than for fashion.

Of course, there were times when gloves were still expected to be worn – for military use, formal occasions such as weddings, funerals and elite social events, and gloves designed specifically for activities such as sport and driving were beginning to be seen.

DRIVING/GOLFING GLOVES

These gloves were usually coloured leather gloves with ventilated palms and, in the case of golf, four round holes at the knuckles for more movement. The driving glove had a woven backing to it and usually a strap around the wrist.

With the rationing after the Second World War, gloves became less important as a social statement, though they did become an important part of fashion. In the 1950s, nylon gloves were popular, often being 'bracelet length', i.e. slightly above the wrist, though very short wrist-length gloves were also seen, and were popular in the 1960s. The 1950s were also the first time you saw faux leather, though the 1960s was when things made of plastic really came to the fore.

Also, after the war, a colour-matching trend came in and it became fashionable to match your hat, gloves, bag and shoes. During the 1940s and 1950s, ladies would not be seen out without their hat and gloves, something that was lost later in the century among the young, except for formal wear.

The 1960s and 1970s also saw cut-out work and appliqué, and gloves became more colourful again.

For the rest of the century, all the above gloves were available, though the material they were made from differed. Driving gloves often had nylon backs, and nylon jersey was used in all forms – silk, satin, lurex, lace or net, especially for evening gloves. There were great improvements in the quality of faux leather, which made these gloves very cheap, though leather gloves were more prized if you could afford them.

There were great innovations in work gloves throughout this century, such as rubber gloves for industrial and housework, latex gloves for medical cleanliness, chainmail gloves for catering and many more. In fact, more gloves were being worn for work than for fashion and that has continued into the twenty-first century.

PROJECT 1 FOUR-PIECE GAUNTLET

Used very early on in the production of gloves, the four-piece gauntlet eliminates the need for fourchettes and helps in the placement of the thumb-piece. It is a loose-fitting glove and not intended to fit exactly, though it can be made bespoke, and with accurate measuring and using finer leather, it can be fitted well and used for fitted gloves and even a decorated sixteenth-century glove; however it is intended to be for an early fighting glove and can be used as a base for a chain-mail or armoured glove which can be added after manufacture. This glove is made for a large man's hand, though it can be altered by measuring the fingers individually, and another measurement from the middle finger to the wrist, and altered to suit. A measurement around the knuckle should also be taken, and the pattern adjusted.

Materials Required

- One sheep's hide, ready dyed (if possible, check for blemishes and unevenness) or equivalent in faux leather
- Leather softener/polish, such as Dubbin
- Thread
- Leather machine-needle
- Any embellishments required

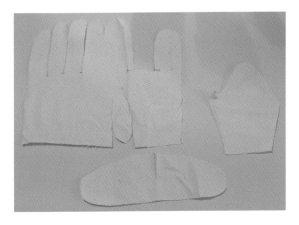

Fig. 4.6 The pattern ready for toile.

Order of Work

1. It is always good to make a toile (a mock-up) of a glove pattern, to make sure it will fit. In this case, as the leather will not be expected to stretch over the hand, the toile may be made using calico or a similar fabric (Figs 4.6 and 4.7).
2. Fit the glove on to the intended wearer and mark on it any alterations needed.
3. Mark the pattern with the alterations.
4. Cut the pattern-pieces out, keeping the leather used as even as possible and avoiding stretched leather as much as possible. Please make sure you do a left and right glove – to do this the pattern-pieces will need to be upside down for one of the gloves. The cut-out pieces are shown in Figs 4.8 and 4.9.
5. Take the thumb-piece and place the corresponding points together, using a 3mm seam.

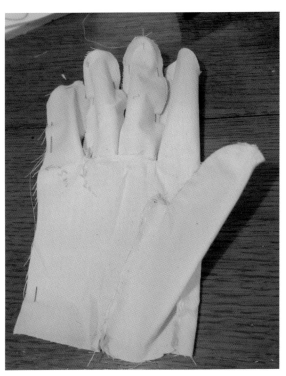

Fig. 4.7 The toile with alterations marked.

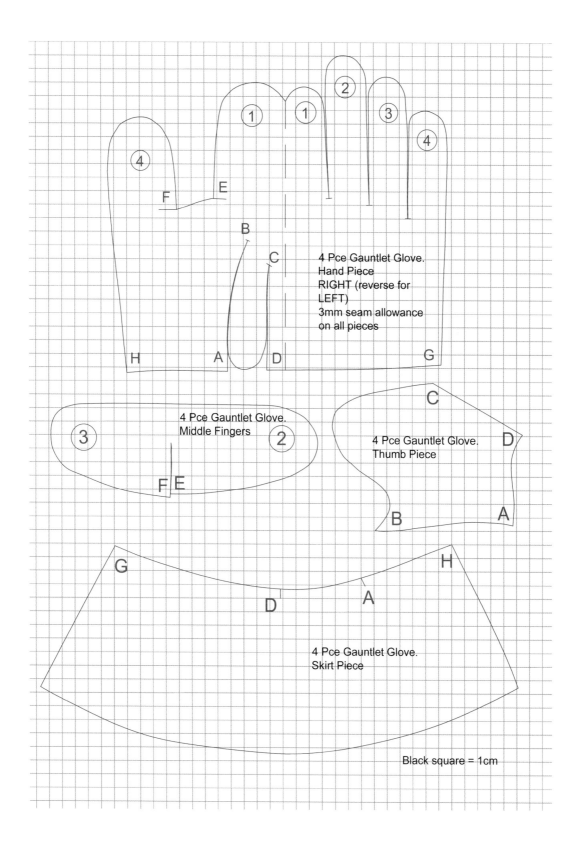

4 Pce Gauntlet Glove.
Hand Piece
RIGHT (reverse for
LEFT)
3mm seam allowance
on all pieces

4 Pce Gauntlet Glove.
Middle Fingers

4 Pce Gauntlet Glove.
Thumb Piece

4 Pce Gauntlet Glove.
Skirt Piece

Black square = 1cm

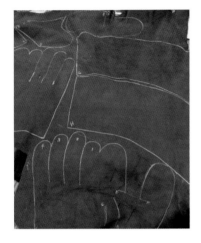

Fig. 4.8 The leather marked out.

Fig. 4.9 The leather cut out.

Fig. 4.10 Sew the thumb in place.

Fig. 4.11 Showing both thumbs.

Fig. 4.12 Attach the skirt.

Fig. 4.13 Finish by sewing round the entire glove.

Fig. 4.14 A leather softener and protector helps to maintain the glove and brings out the colour.

Fig. 4.15 The rivet being pressed in place.

Fig. 4.16 The ring before and after it has been riveted.

6. Carefully sew round the thumb. You may find it easier to do the two sides before easing around the top of the thumb (Figs 4.10 and 4.11).

7. Take the skirt of the glove and sew from G to H on both gloves (Fig. 4.12).

8. Open out the middle fingers pattern-piece and place together points F and E.

9. Sew a 3mm seam from E to F and fold the fingers so that they sit in place.

10. Fold the glove in two and sew from the bottom of the skirt section right around the fingers. This is always easier to do in sections, making sure that the fingers are all aligned. Quilters' clips are useful for this, or fine pins within the seam allowance.

11. Turn the glove through carefully and check over for any missed seams (Fig. 4.13).

12. Rub the gloves with a polish or leather softener to preserve the leather. This should be done periodically through the gloves' life.

Adding Chain Mail

There are many types of split rings that can be used for chain mail, but here we are using steel rings with rivets. This is the most authentic way of making the oldest of chain mail, probably the most fiddly too. These were supplied by 'Ring Lord' of the USA, and they also supplied the rivets and a riveting tool. Each ring needs to be put in position, a rivet placed through the hole and push-riveted together with the tool, as shown in Figs 4.15 and 4.16.

The pattern will depend on the size of your gloves, but this glove used approximately 900 rings. You will also need plenty of extras, as some of the holes are not accurate and you will also have riveting fails.

ORDER OF WORK

1. Open one ring and place two rings on to the ring (these can be previously riveted closed).

Open another ring and take this one through the same two riveting rings. Try and avoid the rings where the hole has gone over the edge, these will not make good links.

2. Carry on until the length of the chain is the width required when it is laid out flat, as in Figs 4.17 and 4.18. If you do another row like this, they can be joined together with a ring.

3. Continue in this way until the chain mail is the length required to cover the glove from the wrist seam to the base of the fingers. This glove required thirty rows to be completed from wrist to finger separation.

> **TIP**
>
> I have found that the rivets are more easily pressed when they are slightly shorter. Going through the rivets and cutting about 1mm off of the ends does make it easier and doesn't reduce the strength of the link.

Dividing for the Fingers

4. Divide the widthways chain into four and leave a chain out at the separations. If you have an uneven number of chains, the smaller finger could be a chain narrower than the other fingers. Please see Figs 4.19 and 4.20.

5. Continue adding rings to each finger until they are the desired length.

6. Figs 4.19 and 4.21 show how to increase the rings to allow the extra width required for the skirt of the gauntlet. This glove required three increase rows resulting in six extra links on the rows.

7. Continue growing the chain mail until it fits the gauntlet skirt. This glove required twenty-six rows to be worked to cover the length of the skirt of the glove.

8. Sew, ideally with fine wire but, alternatively, with strong thread, the chain mail to the gauntlet.

9. If you are storing the gauntlet, a spray of oil helps prevent it from rusting. A de-humidifier, such as a small bag of silica gel, also helps.

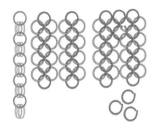

Fig. 4.17 The first row and how two rows are joined.

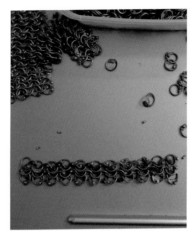

Fig. 4.18 The beginnings of the mail.

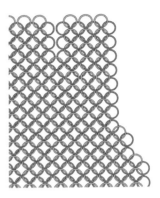

Fig. 4.19 Showing the method of increase and the dividing for the fingers.

Fig. 4.20 The first finger being worked.

Fig. 4.21 The increase ring.

Fig. 4.22 The finished mail.

Fig. 4.23 The mail attached to the glove.

TIP

Sometimes the pattern and process is made clearer and easier by working a few loops before putting the rivets in, though this makes the riveting a little more fiddly.

PROJECT 2 LACE GLOVES

Knotted gloves became popular in the seventeenth century, and crocheting and knitting were also used to achieve a similar result. The example is of a medium size and stretches quite well, though we have given points where the fingers can be lengthened to suit. This pattern assumes some knowledge of crotchet. Everyone crochets with a different tension. Before launching into the pattern, follow the main stitches in a square of at least 5cm and see if it measures the same as the tension given. If it does not, you could either adjust the tightness of your stitch or adjust the pattern accordingly.

This pattern is intended for a Victorian outfit. Extra length could be added to the cuff for earlier or later gloves. The glove pattern and gloves were made by Jude Scott.

Materials Required

- Fine cotton thread, size 20, 385m
- 0.5mm clear, round elastic
- Crochet hook 0.75mm
- Tension 5 spaces to 2.5cm

Throughout you will need to keep trying the glove on and adjust the rows to fit your own hands.

Key ch: chain; tr: treble stitch; ss: slip stitch; st: stitch; sp: space; dc: double crochet.

Order of Work

LEFT HAND

1. Starting at the wrist, crochet 85 ch, ss into the first chain.
2. Row 1: 3 ch, *miss 1 st, 1 tr into next chain, 1 ch*. Repeat from * ending with a ch.
3. Do not join rows.
4. Row 2: 1 tr into space between 3 ch and first tr. *1 ch, 1 tr into next sp , repeat from * to end of row (43 sp).
5. Rows 3–5: *1ch, 1tr into next sp, repeat from* to end.
6. Row 6: Work 1ch, 1tr into the first 3 sp; 1ch, 1tr, 1ch,1tr into the next sp (an increase). Work 1ch, 1tr into the next 4 sp. Work 1ch, 1tr, 1ch, 1tr (another increase) into the next space then 1ch, 1tr into each following sp to the end of the row.
7. Row 7: Work 1ch, 1tr in each sp until the increase in the previous row. Work 1ch, 1tr, 1ch, 1tr into that sp. Work 1ch ,1tr up to the next increase. Work 1ch, 1tr, 1ch, 1tr into that sp. Work 1ch, 1tr to end of the row.
8. Rows 8–19: Repeat row 7, working an increase stitch in the increase spaces of the previous rows.
9. Row 20: Do not increase on this or any subsequent row. Work 1ch, 1tr into every sp until the second increase stitch, 5 ch, 1dc into sp of second increase, 2ch, 1dc into sp over first increase of previous row. This forms the thumb opening. Continue (1ch, 1tr) into each sp to the end of the row (Fig. 4.25).
10. Work 6 more rows of (1ch, tr) sp, bypassing the thumb opening and ending between the ring finger and little finger. When tried on the glove should reach the base of the little finger.
11. Mark off spaces for fingers on the palm and back of the hand. It is best to do this while the glove is on so you may need some help (Fig. 4.26).

Little Finger

12. Work (1ch, 1tr) into each sp round to the marker on the palm side, 4 ch, continue from the marker on the back of the hand 1ch,1tr in each space. Working (1ch, 1tr, 1ch, 1tr) into the 4 ch, continue 1ch, 1tr until finger reaches one row above the base of the fingernail.
13. Work 1tr into each space for one round, then 1ss into each tr.
14. Fasten off, leaving 15cm of thread. Threading a needle with this, draw it through the last row of ss, pull it tight then fasten securely (Fig. 4.27).

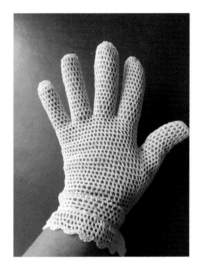

Fig. 4.24 The pattern has been left plain for ease of adding embellishments.

Fig. 4.25 First ten rows, showing the beginning of the increasing for the thumb.

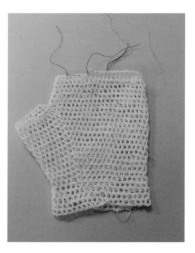

Fig. 4.26 Dividing for the four fingers, marking them with coloured thread is a good way of identifying them without interfering with the crocheting.

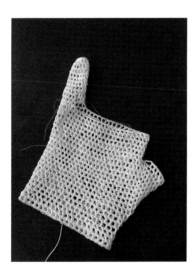

Fig. 4.27 Showing the little figure in place.

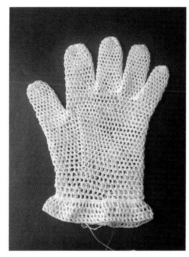

Fig. 4.28 Once the fingers are in place, a small cuff is added.

Ring Finger

15. Attach thread to palm side and work to back of hand until work reaches the little finger. Work around the spaces of the base of the little finger and along the palm side until the marker for the middle finger. Work 5ch and continue round along the back of the hand. Continue and complete as for the little finger.

16. Middle finger: Work as for ring finger, working around the base of the ring finger. Continue as for ring finger.

17. Fore finger: Work as for ring finger, working around the base of the middle finger. Continue as for the other fingers.

18. Thumb: Attach thread to palm side, work around and complete as for other fingers.

Fig. 4.29 Finish off the cuff with a small scallop detail.

Fig. 4.30 the finished gloves by Jude Scott.

Cuff

19. Row 1: Join thread at centre back of the hand. Work over the elastic and into each space as follows: 1dc into same space as join, then 3dc into each sp ending with 2dc into same sp as first dc.
20. Row 2: 4ch, *miss 1dc, 1tr into next dc, 1ch repeat from * ending with 1ss into third of fourth chain.
21. Row 3: 1ss into first sp, 4ch, *1tr into next sp, 1ch, rep from * ending with 1ss into third of 4 ch.
22. Rows 4 and 5: Repeat row 3.
23. Scalloped edge.
24. Worked into the tr st: *ss into first, dc into second, ss into third, 5tr into fourth. Repeat from * to end. Fasten off.

RIGHT HAND

Work as for left hand but making the glove fit the right hand.

Ring Finger

Attach thread to back of the hand and work (1ch, 1tr) until the marker for the middle finger. Work 5ch then work back along the palm side. Continue (1ch, 1tr) as for the little finger.

Middle Finger

Work as for ring finger.

PROJECT 3 LONG GLOVES

Long gloves have been around since the eighteenth century when they were used to cover the bare arms of ladies for the sake of modesty. Most of the time these would have been fine leather or silk, which had to be bespoke to ensure a good fit.

Finely knitted silk gloves were popular throughout the twentieth century and the use of lycra provided a huge improvement in the elasticity of the glove, and, therefore, the cost of manufacture came down and made them more popular for everyone.

These gloves are made from four-way stretch silk jersey. This means that the jersey stretches in both the warp and weft directions. You can also get two-way stretch jersey; in this case, you will need to allow for more length for the fingers. Here, the fourchettes are seamed at the hand end in order to allow for them to be cut on the straight of the fabric and avoid the inevitable twisting otherwise.

Gloves are easier to make using small seam allowances, which is why fabrics that don't fray are generally used. However, if you feel this isn't the case with your fabric, you may need to bind or use a fray-check on the edges. These gloves are made for a medium size.

Materials Required

- 0.5m of four-way stretch jersey silk satin
- A small amount of silk (or other lightweight fabric) for the buttonholes and facing
- 6 × 10mm buttons
- Thread
- Ball point or jersey machine needles

Order of Work

1. Cut all the pattern-pieces out in the jersey fabric, following the straight of grain marks. Make sure you mark each fourchette with the corresponding finger to avoid confusion later.
2. Cut four pieces of fabric for the facings of the button and buttonholes, 10 × 4cm. Neaten the edges, if necessary.
3. Mark on two of the facings, three 1cm long buttonholes, 2cm apart (heat-sensitive pens are ideal for this).
4. Tack into position on the right side of the fabric and sew with a machine, from one end of the mark to the other, coming out 2mm on either side. Try and do this in one go, twisting the work round at the tip of the buttonhole. This

Fig. 4.31 Place in position using pattern.

Fig. 4.32 Tack carefully in place.

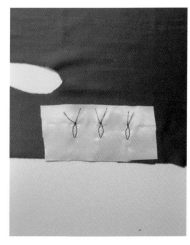

Fig. 4.33 Knot the ends of the thread.

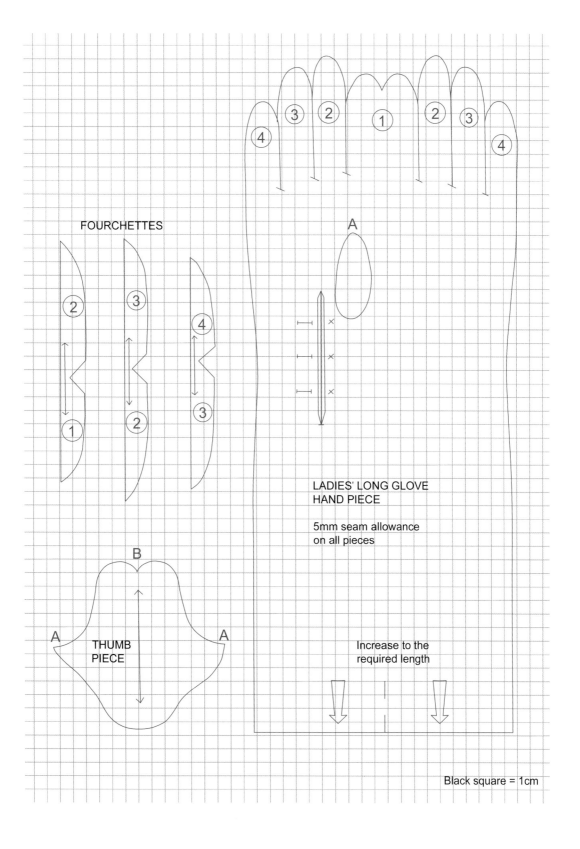

FOURCHETTES

A

LADIES' LONG GLOVE
HAND PIECE

5mm seam allowance
on all pieces

B

A   A

THUMB
PIECE

Increase to the
required length

Black square = 1cm

will allow them to be sniped right into the corner, as shown in Fig. 4.33.

5. Cut the facing in between the buttonholes and turn through to the other side.

6. Press the facing right out to the seam (Fig. 4.34) and then bring the seam allowances towards the centre, folding the facing back out and pressing, making the sides of the buttonhole.

7. Prick stitch through around the edge of the buttonholes to keep them in place.

8. Take the other two facing pieces and neaten around the edge; this could be bound or overlocked, whichever is more appropriate, taking into account that this will be seen and needs to be robust.

9. Place along the marked line and tack in place.

10. Machine sew from the top of the mark to the bottom, coming out 2mm on either side as with the buttonholes.

NOTE

At each end, curve the stitching out 2mm quickly, as if it is graduated too finely, the seam allowance will become too small when cut.

11. Cut along the centre of the stitching, right into the corners at either end, making sure you don't cut the thread.

12. Turn through the facing to the other side and press in place. (If this looks slightly stretched, as in Fig. 4.38, this is fine, it will allow the glove to stretch on the hand.)

13. Take the thumb-pieces, fold in half and sew along the inside edge (Fig. 4.39).

14. Place in position and machine sew in place, using a small zigzag or stretch stitch (Fig. 4.40).

NOTE

I strongly suggest that at this point and beyond, you tack the pieces in position first; this will make sure that the fabric does not stretch differently and result in twisting.

15. Take the fourchettes and pair up 1+2, 2+3, 3+4; sew along the lower edge on each (Fig. 4.41).

16. Tack these in place on to the glove (Fig. 4.42) and machine stitch in place. Remove the tacking.

17. Turn the glove through and sew the buttons in place.

Fig. 4.34 Snip along the buttonhole right into the corners.

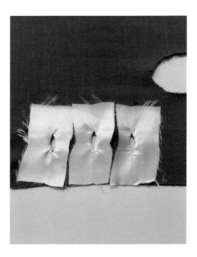

Fig. 4.35 Press flat first to get a crisper finish.

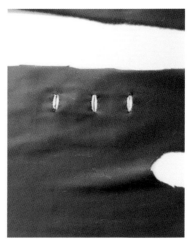

Fig. 4.36 Bring the flaps back either side and stitch.

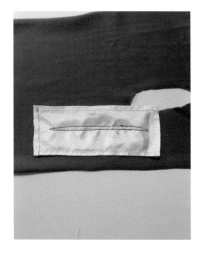

Fig. 4.37 Tack facing in position carefully.

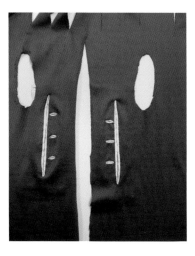

Fig. 4.38 The finished buttonholes and slit.

Fig. 4.39 Finish ends of thumb seams off securely.

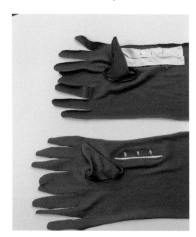

Fig. 4.40 Turn through at each stage to ensure correct positioning.

Fig. 4.41 Ensure that you are attaching the correct fourchettes.

Fig. 4.42 Tacking first ensures even stretch of the fabric.

Fig. 4.43 Turn through and press.

Fig. 4.44 Turn up the hem and fold it back on itself.

Fig. 4.45 The finished hem.

HEMMING THE GLOVES

18. Turn the hem of the glove over to the desired length, then fold them back on themselves to the edge of the hem (Fig. 4.45).

19. Zigzag or overlock around the edge and fold of the fabric together (move the cutting blade out of the way).

20. This creates a worked cuff. (Alternatively, you could work a closely stitched herringbone stitch.)

Fig. 4.46 The finished gloves.

5
JEWELLERY

INTRODUCTION AND HISTORY

Jewellery describes the adornment of a costume or body and, although it is usually merely for decoration, it also often had a practical purpose; for example, the penannulars of medieval times, which were used to hold drapes together.

It is difficult to make an exact study of the complete history of jewellery. Digs at prehistoric burial sites and dwellings have given ideas of jewellery that existed at the time, especially in items made from materials with longevity, such as metals; however, it was, and still is in many cultures, without doubt, true that people adorn themselves with jewellery made from materials available from the local area, such as plants, flowers, bones, leather and wood. In history, many of these items would have been lost due to their biodegradable nature. Widespread travel, discovery of different cultures, international trading and colonization did, of course, distribute local crafts; however, there is still local traditional and religious jewellery that exist within cultures all around the world.

When researching for a play it is always advisable to study the area in which the play is set, the religions and the local resources available to the indigenous people of the area, as well as any visitors to the area and what they might have brought with them as personal jewellery. For the purposes of this introduction, we will be concentrating on the jewellery of Britain, Ireland, Scotland and surrounding islands.

Medieval and Before

By 325BC Britain was known to be mining tin, copper and gold. It was exported across Europe

Fig. 5.1 Showing the mechanics of a pennanular.

Fig. 5.2 Showing some chatelaines. The one of the left is a Victorian housemaid's chatelaine. Also shown is a Victorian silver glasses' case and a small silver bag.

and may well have contributed to the start of the Bronze Age (3300–1200BC, arguably up to AD500). Most of the tin and copper mines were in Cornwall and Wales, with gold in Wales and Ireland.

Then came the Iron Age and the invasion and settlements of (among others) the Normans and Romans, followed by Germanic settlers and Viking invasions, all bringing their own metals and styles from Europe. The Saxons brought big, square-shaped brooches and the Germanic invasions brought the animal art to the Celtic interwoven lines. Until the later medieval times, jewels were rounded (cabochon) rather than faceted (1250–1500).

Most of the jewellery throughout medieval times had a practical use – be it closing a tunic or wrap – or a medical or spiritual use. The style of jewellery was very closely related to religion, luck or love. The stones used were also often chosen for their supposed healing or fertility powers. Many pieces were very exquisitely engraved with script or enamelled with detailed sacred scenes.

Penannulars, or Celtic brooches, were used from early medieval times as clothing fasteners. They were often a crucial closure, especially when the clothing consisted of just a flat piece of cloth, draped around the body. They consisted of a loop of metal, with a gap that a pin can fit; the pin is attached to the loop with a tube so that the pin can move freely. The pin is put through the cloth and stopped from becoming loose by moving the loop around under the pin and away from the gap. They could be very basic and functional or highly decorated on either side of the gap and at the head of the pin. The penannular is found in many cultures, including North African tribes and Scottish clansmen. It was worn by both men and women.

Wedding rings were part of the Christian marriage ceremony and started being worn in AD900, having probably previously been introduced by the Ancient Romans. They came in many forms and during the late medieval times were often quite ornate, as they also were seen as part of the dowry of the marriage. For this reason, they were worn by the wife.

Sixteenth Century

The Renaissance brought many new designers and much more money was spent on adornment generally. Christopher Columbus also discovered South America in 1492 so the trade of emeralds and pearls, as well as gold and silver, brought many precious items to British shores via Spain, which influenced jewellery a great deal.

Pendants were very popular and many were very ornate, with large stones carved into animals or other things relevant to the wearer, such as ships, held by ornate gold settings, often enamelled.

Later in the sixteenth century, the pendants were more symmetrical and the settings tended to be scrollwork, with the stones either screwed or riveted into place. Cameo carving was also popular; the stones would be engraved with initials, faces, coat of arms or animals.

Rings were also made with large stones, often engraved and used as a seal and sometimes with a hinged opening to conceal a potion or memory of someone (a tooth or lock of hair). Much of the significance of the stones used was still relevant in this century, either as an aid to prayer or to ward off evil spirits and also as an aid to health.

During this time, wedding rings were often in different parts. Either they were worn by both partners during engagement and formed part of the ceremony to be worn together on the wife's finger, or in the form of a puzzle ring (rendering it difficult to remove and return). These endured longer in Europe.

The second half of the sixteenth century saw longer, elaborately jewelled chains. The fashion of ruffs had required longer chains, also beads, as shown in many portraits of Elizabeth I.

Seventeenth Century

Many of the influences from the Renaissance still remain, including the gold and silver ornamentation. The second half saw more French influences in all areas of fashion, with men beginning to wear watches, rings and buckles. Women had pins, earrings, bracelets and rings. In everyday use, these were not ornate, often made with gold and pearls, with more elaborate stones being worn for more formal events. Enamel was often a feature in jewellery.

Elizabeth I's liking for pearls endured, and both pearls and drop-pearl earrings were popular, as well as tear-shaped drop stones of all types. Bows matching the bodice were often worn at the top of the stomacher, held in place by a brooch.

Eighteenth Century

Pearls were still being worn; however, they were more elaborate with additional stones and gems. Tippets finishing the cords and ribbons of the stomacher, skirts and dress fastenings became more ornate.

Steel was used for the first time to make jewellery, and gradually became valued for its beauty. Men would have their buttons highly polished, as reflected in many writings of the time.

Baroque styles of the early eighteenth century were influenced by the increased travel of the late eighteenth century, bringing the Rococo style, with softer, curved lines.

Large pendants were fashionable towards the end of the century, with beautifully enamelled miniatures. These pieces of jewellery were often worn in memory of a lost love and could have a compartment in the back containing a plait of hair. Hair was also used to embroider or frame such an item.

After the French revolution in the later part of the century, and the emergence of the neoclassical fashion of empire-line dresses, chokers and ornate beaded necklaces worn high on the neck and draping down into the cleavage of the dresses were very popular. These necklaces could be made from any materials ranging from glass or stone to precious or semi-precious gems.

The eighteenth century was also the time when 'paste' jewellery was very popular and well thought of, thanks to innovations made and brought over from France. This allowed jewellery to be available to the masses, though also accepted by all, as many of the top jewellers were using it.

Nineteenth Century

The nineteenth century was known for silver jewellery, which was worked in very fine and delicate ways. However, many other materials were used in the manufacture of jewellery. Steel made a resurgence and was cut and polished and made into chains and chatelaines.

CHATELAINES
Chatelaines were made to hook over the waistband, and the hook had several carrying holes from which hung several chains that could hold items useful to the wearer. For example, a gaoler might carry keys, while a housekeeper might have sewing equipment, thimble, needle case, scissors, even a pin cushion. They might also be for carrying glasses or a dance card. The chains could be metal or leather, or even ribbons, and the hook at the top could be very ornate or rather plain. Chatelaines are used all over the world and there are many shown in museums and in art.

At the beginning of the century, high-necked beaded necklaces were still popular, though they were replaced by delicate pendants, including those of a religious nature (crosses or stars), delicate stones or lockets.

LOCKETS
Having already been used in rings, the pendant necklace was first seen in the seventeenth century and has been used as a pomade, to hold good-luck charms, pictures and locks of hair and, more lately, medical history and information. However, their most popular time was during the nineteenth century when they were used for all the above and could be engraved, enamelled, encrusted with jewels or a combination of all three. They could be very small or gaudily large. Small lockets were often given to bridesmaids as

keepsakes and have always had an association with memorabilia.

Silver was very evident and women wore a lot of jewellery, especially brooches. Necklaces and earrings didn't necessarily match. The high necks of the late nineteenth century brought the fashion of a cameo or jewelled brooch worn at the neck.

HANDICRAFT GUILD

Towards the end of the century, the Handicraft Guild was formed. It sought to revive some traditional crafts of the past and the artists were self-taught, bringing a freshness to their commercially made pieces.

Twentieth Century

ART NOUVEAU

Right at the beginning of the century was born the art nouveau style. Named after a shop in Paris, it presented more fluid lines, with subjects closer to nature, with leaves and flowers brought to life in silver or gold, and often enamelled, including 'plique-à-jour', which is a way of enamelling that spans an open frame, allowing the light to flow through the piece. The colours are pastel, resembling the natural colours of the subject.

Throughout the twentieth century, jewellery became more co-ordinated, with matching necklaces and earrings becoming a must. Pearls were particularly fashionable through the first half of the century. Jewellery was abundant, though quite modest, except for that worn by the young during the 1920s and again in the 1960s, when a blast of colour and plastic provided exciting and large jewellery pieces.

ART DECO

Between the 1920s and 1935, there was a 'cubism' style of jewellery, later known as art deco. The geometric designs were usually worked in silver or platinum, encrusted with diamonds and often cabochons of jade or other semi-precious stones,

Twenty-First Century

At the beginning of the twenty-first century, all the traditional forms of jewellery were still available and many people wore the jewellery that most suited their character. There was a nostalgia for Victorian jewellery.

Experimentation into using different materials and methods of manufacture, including plastics, knitted silver, cast silver and leather saw a craft look to fashionable jewellery. Flowers and nature were again in vogue.

PROJECT 1 WEDDING RINGS

Keeping a supply of wedding rings is an important part of wardrobe stock. They are also the item of costume prop that gets lost most often. I encourage actors to have one for themselves, which they know fits well, in their kit.

You can buy cheap 'wedding rings' and these are good if you can get the correct size. However, often they cannot be stretched and are also quite light and may not give the correct feeling for the actor.

There are very cheap options, which we can investigate later in this chapter; however, first, we shall look at making a wedding ring out of brass. Brass gives a very good impression of gold and even though it needs polishing every now and then, it remains an excellent option.

This ring is made for a finger of size 57.

Fig. 5.3 Some of the sizing equipment available.

Materials Required

- 70mm 'D'-profile brass rod
- Ring sizer (if one is not available, measure the ring by wrapping a strip of paper, the same width as the brass, around the finger and measuring this)
- A ring mandrel
- A ring-sizing mandrel
- A vice
- A piercing saw
- A ring stretcher (optional)
- A soft hammer (a bit of weight to the hammer is also required, so a wooden mallet is of less use.)
- Pliers (jewellers' pliers have no gripping teeth; these can be removed from ordinary pliers by filing)
- A blowtorch (a butane one will suffice)
- Silver-solder and flux (or silver-solder paste)
- Various grades of abrasive paper (a polishing wheel for a drill or polishing machine is also useful)

Fig. 5.4 A solid steel mandrel and a sizing mandrel (the sizing mandrel is hollow and not appropriate for shaping the ring).

Order of Work

1. Cut 62mm of the brass (using the saw will allow for a straighter edge and help the process).
2. Make sure the ends are flat and at right angles to the length.
3. Anneal the brass using the blowtorch. To do this, heat the strip evenly by moving the blowtorch constantly along it until it becomes a cherry-red colour, and leave to cool. This will make the strip more pliable. (Annealing the metal aligns the molecules within the metal;

Fig. 5.5 Measuring the D-strip.

Fig. 5.6 Ensure that the ends are level and square.

Fig. 5.7 Heat to an even cherry-red colour.

Fig. 5.8 Put the mandrel in a vice before hitting is the safest way.

Fig. 5.9 Using a hard plastic or specialist jewellers' mallet ensures that you don't mark the ring.

Fig. 5.10 The shaped ring on the mandrel.

these will get rearranged again while working with the metal, so it will become gradually more difficult to bend. It can be annealed several times during a lengthy smithing job.)

4. Place the ring mandrel in a vice and hit the strip into a circle using the soft-tipped hammer (it doesn't matter if it isn't perfectly round).
5. Bring the ends of the strip together using your pliers – be careful not to mark the brass. Make sure you get a joint with no gaps. (Jewellers' pliers don't have the 'teeth' that normal pliers have, for this reason.)
6. Place a small amount of solder paste to the inside of the ring.
7. Heat the ring from the outside using the blowtorch until you see the solder coming through the joint.
8. At this point, you could put the ring into pickle to help remove the discoloration.
9. File the joint until it is smooth (don't forget the inside).
10. Using fine-grade abrasive paper, remove any marks from the brass.
11. Polish the ring to a high shine.

Stretching a Ring

There are many ring stretchers on the market, some of which are shown in Figs 5.3 and 5.14. If none of these is available to you, and your ring is too small, you can stretch a ring by annealing it, placing it on the mandrel and hitting it with the soft hammer until it is forced down the shaft, so making it bigger. To get it off again, hit it from below, so dislodging it.

Using Patterned Strips

There are many pattern strips available, especially in copper. These might lend themselves well to older wedding rings and are very easy to use.

ORDER OF WORK

1. Either using paper, or the strip itself, work out the size that the ring needs to be.
2. Wrap the strip round on itself to the required size.

Fig. 5.11 Move the edges together using pliers – you can flatten the shape of the ring at this point and reshape after soldering.

Fig. 5.12 Solder the ends together.

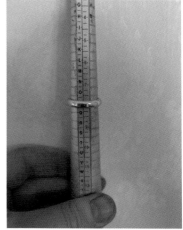

Fig. 5.13 The finished ring after polishing.

3. With an eye on the pattern on the ring, pick a place where the pattern matches and saw through both parts of the strip using a piercing saw. The cuts should match and fit together perfectly (see Figs 5.16–5.19).
4. Place the ring on a heat-proof surface (I usually carve a groove in the surface to help hold the ring in the correct position for soldering – see Fig. 5.20).

5. Place a small amount of solder paste on the inside of the joint and heat from the outside, as we did with the D-section brass.
6. The copper will discolour, but do not worry, it will polish up – the main thing is that the joint is good. The ring can now go in the pickle, where it will lose the blackness and turn slightly pink.
7. Fig. 5.23 shows half the ring being polished and the difference it makes.
8. Continue polishing the ring to a good shine.

Fig. 5.14 A cheaper and easy-to-use ring stretcher.

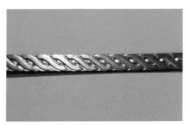

Fig. 5.15 An example of a patterned brass strip.

Fig. 5.16 Sizing the ring.

Fig. 5.17 Pattern match before cutting.

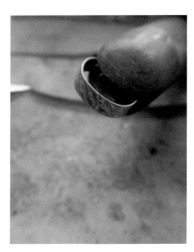

Fig. 5.18 and Fig. 5.19 The pattern matched.

Fig. 5.20 Place in a heatproof brick and secure in position.

Fig. 5.21 Soldering the joint.

Fig. 5.22 The piece is bound to discolour at this point (if it is to be an ancient ring, you might like to polish it from here and get an interesting patina).

Fig. 5.23 The piece pickled and half-polished.

Fig. 5.24 The finished, polished piece.

Making Rings out of Plumber's Olives

The olives that plumbers use to seal pipes make an extremely cheap alternative to making brass rings. They are especially good for making a wider man's ring. They are limited to size but can be stretched or cut and soldered to make smaller. If you are lucky enough to need to make a Y-size ring (12.25 US), a standard 22mm olive will fit perfectly. Fig. 5.25 shows a selection of olives in their raw state. Fig. 5.26 shows the difference when the ring has been filed down and polished up.

Fig. 5.25 Plumber's olives.

Fig. 5.26 The finished ring next to the original olive.

PROJECT 2 SOVEREIGN RING

First produced in the fifteenth century, a sovereign was produced as a commemorative item when a sovereign was crowned, a ring bearing a coin being placed on the sovereign's finger during the service. Sovereign rings were more widely worn during the nineteenth century and since sovereign coins are solid gold, have been placed in many jewellery items and bought as an investment.

This particular way of making a 'sovereign-type' ring can be used for setting any stone or gem that is flat-backed. We have used a pound coin, which is roughly the size of a sovereign and, of course, somewhat cheaper. The ring is made from brass, which, when polished, mimics gold very well.

Materials Required

- Enough 1mm brass sheet to accommodate the pattern (I used an offcut)
- Paper and marker (a soft pencil works well)
- A pound coin
- A piercing saw
- A jewellers' peg (as shown in Fig. 5.32) and a vice with smooth jaws

- A selection of fine files and various grades of abrasive paper
- A polishing wheel or small mop attached to a drill
- A soft hammer
- Heat-proof mats or a hearth
- A blowtorch (butane torches are fine, though a large flame is required when heating the whole piece)
- A ring mandrel
- Silver-solder and flux or ready-mixed solder paste.
- Jewellers' pickle (various types available)

Order of Work

1. Measure around the coin, then halve this measurement. Measure around the finger and create a pattern as shown in Fig. 5.27, where the curved edge is the same length as the finger circumference and the flat edge is the measurement of half the circumference of the coin.
2. Check your pattern by taping the ring around the coin and trying on the finger or ring mandrel (Figs 5.28 and 5.29).
3. Mark on the brass and carefully cut out the shape using a piercing saw and peg. Smooth

Fig. 5.27 A paper pattern for the ring.

Fig. 5.28 Fitting the pattern to the coin.

Fig. 5.29 Fitting the pattern to the finger.

the edges with a file, making sure the straight edges remain straight (Figs 5.30–5.33).

4. Mark round the coin on another piece of brass and cut this out, smoothing the edge until it is exactly the size and shape of the coin (Figs 5.34–5.37).

5. Anneal the main piece of metal (Fig. 5.38).

> **TIP**
>
> When filing a straight edge, it is very easy to round the edges accidently. Holding the piece in a vice with the edge just showing above the jaws and then filing to the top of the vice jaws is an accurate way of keeping them straight.

Fig. 5.30 Mark the pattern on a piece of brass.

Fig. 5.31 Cutting the pattern out using a piercing saw and jewellers' peg. This allows the worker to be in control of both the brass and the saw, safely.

Fig. 5.32 The piece cut out.

Fig. 5.33 Smooth out any saw marks with a file – move the file across the work diagonally, along the brass, to ensure a smooth finish.

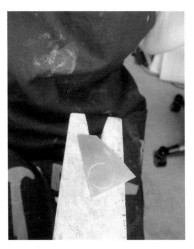

Fig. 5.34 Mark another piece of brass with the coin.

Fig. 5.35 Cut out the disc using a piercing saw and jewellers' peg.

ANNEALING

Annealing is heating the metal up until it is evenly red hot; this aligns the molecules of the metal, which makes it more malleable and easier to work. With brass, the metal should be heated to a cherry red and left to cool; it can also be quenched in water to cool. While working it (filing and shaping), the metal can harden again, so often, when jewellery making, the metal is annealed more than once through the process.

6. Shape the ring around a mandrel, both the coin setting and ring. A soft hammer should be used for this, which will not mark the metal (Figs 5.39 and 5.40). Make sure the edges of the setting are straight and fit together well.
7. Place a small amount of solder on the inside of the setting and heat from the outside with the blowtorch until the solder is seen to come through the joint (Fig. 5.41).

> **NOTE**
>
> From this point, the metal will discolour badly; this is normal and will normalize with pickling/polishing.

8. Rub down the join with fine abrasive paper and reshape on the mandrel (Figs 5.42 and 5.43).
9. Place the coin-shaped disc into the setting, about 1mm below the depth of the coin. This might take more filing. Ideally you want the disc to be 'push fit' into place.
10. Place a small amount of solder around the disc, on the ring side, and heat from the top until the solder melts through the joint (Fig. 5.45).
11. Drill a small hole in the middle of the disc; this has a purely practical purpose – it makes it easier to remove the coin if need be at a later date.
12. Pickle the piece (Fig. 5.46).

PICKLING

Picking is a fluid that can be either acid or alkali. Leaving the piece in pickle removes the discoloration due to oxidization and flame damage. It can be very toxic, but kinder solutions are also available, e.g. citric acid.

13. File the edge of the top of the setting to a 45-degree angle (Fig. 5.45).
14. Place the coin in the void created and bang the edge over with a planishing hammer or

Fig. 5.36 Smooth out any saw marks with a file, moving the file around the shape of the disc to ensure a smooth finish.

Fig. 5.37 Ensure the disc is the same size as the coin.

Fig. 5.38 Anneal, making sure that you keep the flame moving over the whole piece to ensure you do not overheat one section.

Fig. 5.39 Shape the finger section over a mandrel.

Fig. 5.40 Shape the coin section over the mandrel, refinishing the edges so that they fit together perfectly.

Fig. 5.41 Solder both the joints by putting solder paste on the inside and heating from the outside.

Fig. 5.42 File the joint smooth.

Fig. 5.43 Reshape the ring.

Fig. 5.44 Make sure the ring is the right size – the ring section can be filed slightly larger at this point.

setting tool. The edge of the tool should be smooth, otherwise serious marks on the edge will be difficult to remove (Fig. 5.48).

15. File into shape and polish (Figs 5.49 and 5.50).

POLISHING

Polishing can be done by rubbing the piece with ever-reducing grades of abrasive paper, followed by some silver polish. However, by far the most effective polishing method – possibly as well as the above – is to use a polishing wheel (either purpose-made or a small attachment to a dremel, as in Fig. 5.49). To make the polishing effective, apply some jewellers' rouge to the polishing cloth before using.

Another way to further polish a piece is to put it in a rolling polisher, filled with stainless-steel shot pellets. This will planish and polish the piece and can be used in conjunction with the other polishing methods.

Fig. 5.45 Position the disc in the ring – to get the exact position, put the coin in too and ensure that the ring is about 1mm above the coin.

Fig. 5.46 The pickling will make the piece a pink colour – this is normal.

Fig. 5.47 Bevel the edge.

Fig. 5.48 Turn the edge over, all the way round. It might not appear smooth to start with but working it round will help.

Fig. 5.49 Polishing with a dremel – note the heat-proof gloves – the ring will get very hot at this point.

Fig. 5.50 The finished ring.

PROJECT 3 RESTRINGING PEARLS

Knotting pearls is an extremely useful skill to learn. Many of the vintage pearls you either have been given or come across at sales are broken; restringing them gives them a new life and also makes them more robust for the stage.

Of course, this skill can be used for any beads and you can see how useful it would be to prevent any beaded necklace from breaking and scattering on stage.

Fig. 5.51 Some of the range of silk sizes.

Choosing the Thread

There are synthetic and silk threads that are suitable for stringing. Other natural fine threads are not really strong enough and will wear in time. If, however, you are stringing beads with large holes, a waxed, natural thread works well.

The thread should fit the hole of the bead well, otherwise the knot will pass through the hole and be useless. However, the thread should be able to pass through the bead twice, so the thickness of the thread is important to get right.

Fig. 5.52 Showing the grown-on needle on the silk.

Choosing the Needle

There are two types of beading needle: one with a fine eye at one end and another that has an eye the whole length of the needle. The latter is easier to thread, though is not so strong. They both come in multiple sizes and, of course, should pass through the bead easily. When buying silk for re-threading, many have a needle already attached, which allows the maximum possible thickness of thread to go through the pearls easily.

Fig. 5.53 The donor pearls – the string appears to have stretched or a pearl has broken.

Materials Required

- A donor broken necklace or the required number of beads to make the necklace of your choice, plus fastenings
- An appropriate thread
- An appropriate needle
- A small amount of French wire (or gimp)
- Fine scissors
- Either jewellers' glue or a heat source (lighter or purpose-made torch)

Preparation

Preparing the Beads

Dismantle the beads and lay them in the same order that they were strung. Find a tray with an indent or some fabric with texture, so that they don't roll. Thread these beads on to the thread (allow at least four times the length of the necklace to allow for the knotting) (Fig. 5.54).

> **NOTE**
>
> Natural pearls come in many sizes and are sorted so that the same sizes are strung together, even when they all look the same size overall. Often they get larger towards the middle, but either way it is easier to keep the same order.

Stretching the Silk

Silk thread is heavily twisted and comes tightly wrapped. It is good practice to let it relax and also allow it to stretch to its natural length. Tie the end of the thread back on to the card it came on, dampen the thread slightly and hang on a hook overnight. If your beads are very small, you can add further, larger beads to the loop, but do not overload it, it should be a gentle stretch.

Fig. 5.54 Take the strong out – be very careful to keep them in order.

Fig. 5.55 Stretching the silk overnight.

Order of Work

1. Make sure the beads are secured on to the thread, knotting a bead on to the end and work from the other end of the thread.
2. Bring the first bead up from the row.
3. Cut 1cm of French gimp and thread this on to the end of the thread.
4. Take the thread through the bead again and knot the threads together.

5. Bring the next bead up the thread so that it sits tight up against the first.
6. Make a knot, as shown in Figs 5.63 and 5.65.
7. Move the knot up the thread towards the second bead with a spare needle, as shown.
8. Continue bringing the beads up and knotting the thread, until all the beads have been knotted, apart from one.
9. Move this bead up and thread another 1cm length of French gimp on to the end.
10. Take the thread through the last bead again and pull the bead up loosely to the second-to last bead.
11. Tie the thread round the main thread between the last two beads.

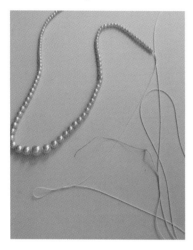

Fig. 5.56 Thread all the beads on the silk. Allow extra thread for the knots to be made.

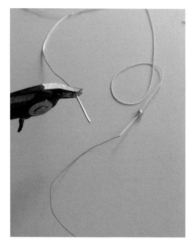

Fig. 5.57 One bead on the thread and cutting 1cm of gimp.

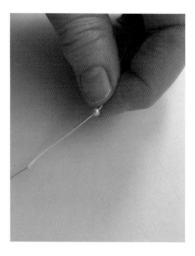

Fig. 5.58 Thread the gimp on to the silk.

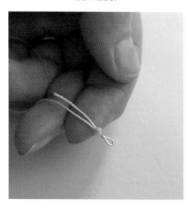

Fig. 5.59 Thread the silk back through the bead, forming a loop.

Fig. 5.60 Tie a knot against the bead.

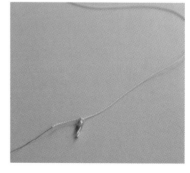

Fig. 5.61 It is important that this knot is tight up against the bead, though the other knots need to be a bit looser to allow the movement of the necklace.

12. Place a small amount of jewellers' glue on to this, and the first knot or melt the ends of the thread using a small flame or a purpose-made thread burner.
13. Add a jump ring to each loop of French gimp and attach to the clasp.

TIP

You can buy a 'threading tool' that is designed to knot the thread and get it close to the bead; one of these is shown in Fig. 5.64.

Fig. 5.62 The next pearl goes on to just the main thread.

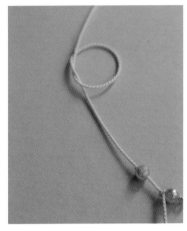

Fig. 5.63 Tie the next knot.

Fig. 5.64 Using the knotting tool. It holds the thread up against the pearl as you tighten it.

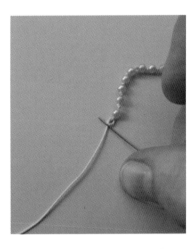

Fig. 5.65 Using a needle to do the same job, move the knot against the pearl.

Fig. 5.66 Continue in this way until you have one pearl left.

Fig. 5.67 Thread the last bead on without knotting.

Fig. 5.68 Thread another 1cm gimp on to the end of the thread.

Fig 5.71 Completed pearl string attached to a clasp with jump rings.

Fig. 5.69 Take the thread through the last bead and tie between the last two beads.

Fig. 5.70 Put a tiny drop of jewellers' glue on the last knot on each end.

PROJECT 4 IMPROVING CHEAP JEWELLERY

There is an amazing amount of very cheap jewellery available both on the internet and on the high street. Many are excellent shapes and styles, though let themselves down once they are under light. However, there are often ways to improve these items and make them a lot more authentic-looking.

Improving a Cheap Necklace

Budgets are often low in small theatre productions and there are a lot of cheap alternatives to authentic pearls and expensive beads. However, they are often obviously cheap but there are simple ways of improving the look. We will also use another method to knot the thread, which is slightly quicker than the previous method discussed.

AIM
- To improve the colour and look of the beads.
- To re-thread to allow the necklace to hang correctly and make it more secure.

MATERIALS REQUIRED
- Appropriate thread. Ideally, you would use fine silk or synthetic thread specifically sold for threading beads. However, the holes in these beads were so large that I used leatherwork thread in order to keep the beads in place.
- A donor necklace
- Jewellers' glue

ORDER OF WORK
1. Unthread the beads and put the fastenings aside.
2. Sort the beads. In this case, I made sure that there were more beads for the lower string, to allow them to fall better.
3. Cut a length of thread, twice the length of one side of the top row of pearls.
4. In this case, we have a centre-piece, so fold the thread in half and pass it through the loop of the centre-piece. Take the thread through and secure it, as shown in Fig. 5.73.
5. Take both threads through the next bead and knot the threads together, as shown in Figs 5.74, 5.75 and 5.76.
6. Continue like this until all the beads on one side are knotted, except one.

Fig. 5.72 This necklace would scream plastic under lights, though the setting is nice and can be improved very easily.

Fig. 5.73 Tie the double thread by looping it through the setting hole and running the thread through the loop formed.

Fig. 5.74 Tie the thread together and put both threads through the next bead.

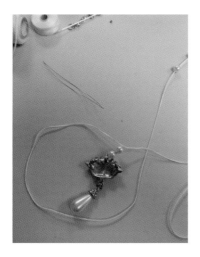

Fig. 5.75 Add another bead and tie another knot.

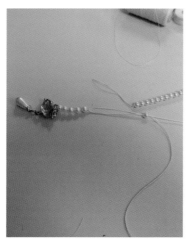

Fig. 5.76 Continue the process until the required beads are threaded.

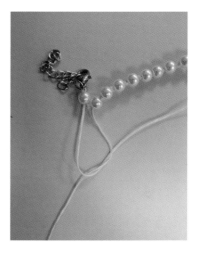

Fig. 5.77 Tie to the fastening by passing one thread through the last bead and the loop of the fastening. Tie a knot, then pass it back through the last bead.

Fig. 5.78 Tie to the other thread.

Fig. 5.79 Only use a few crystals of the potassium permanganate.

Fig. 5.80 Check continually, it is very easy to go too far.

7. Take one thread through the last bead and knot it around the loop of the fastening.
8. Take the thread through the last bead and knot to the other thread, as shown in Figs 5.77 and 5.78.
9. Secure this with jewellers' glue.
10. Carry out the same process on the other rows of pearls.

COLOURING THE NECKLACE

11. Take a quarter of a teaspoon of potassium permanganate and put it into hot water (not boiling) (Fig. 5.79).
12. Place the necklace in the mixture, checking constantly until it is the required colour (Fig. 5.80).

Fig. 5.81 shows the difference in colour you should try and achieve. It also shows how the pearls sit well next to each other and also a slight colouring of the 'metal' setting, which ages the necklace well.

Metal-Plating Jewellery

Occasionally it is useful to be able to transform a base metal to look like a precious metal when making a prop or even a specific piece of jewellery. An example of this is the cane with the wolf's head printed handle, shown in Chapter 7, where the copper sleeve over the spigot joining the handle to the cane needed to be silver. There are three fundamental ways of doing this.

PAINT OR LACQUER

If this is done well, with a carefully selected, suitable paint, this can most certainly be a viable option. There are a great range of paints available now – many, of course, aerosols, which require ventilation and care to get a good finish. Metals usually require priming before painting, although there are some paints that will 'key' or self-etch on to a surface without primer – they are the exception. An application of paint can also hide fine detail due to the build-up of layers.

PLATING SOLUTIONS

Silver-plating solution is available affordably for the plating of brass, copper, nickel and bronze. This is a very good product and the next best thing to magic. It is bought in a 150ml bottle and used thus:

Fig. 5.81 Comparing the original (right) against what we have achieved.

Fig. 5.82 The new, improved necklace.

First, clean the surface of the item to be plated by giving it a quick polish. Then, after shaking the bottle, pour a little of the contents on to a clean cloth and liberally apply to the work surface. Darkening will occur as the transfer of silver takes place. Finally, buff lightly with a soft cloth to a nice shine.

This liquid only works on copper-based metals (such as those listed above). The sleeve on the wolf's head cane was treated with this solution, as was the clasp on the chain-mail bag.

ELECTROPLATING

Electroplating can be outsourced to a large number of local companies, though there are companies who specialize in polishing and electroplating props for film and television, such as BJS of Perivale, West London; or, if you are feeling brave, it can be undertaken domestically (on a small scale).

Our interest is likely to be focused on props appearing to be copper, silver and gold, rather than the various other colours, such as red, green, blue and so on, which can be obtained by anodizing aluminium. This may also be achieved at a 'domestic' level but since it involves the use of acid and is less likely to be of use, we will not cover anodizing here. The process is readily available commercially, and easily researched, if desired.

Electroplating of copper and gold, however, is of some use. There is a plethora of cheap jewellery available (particularly from China) made from cheap alloy, of useful form but poor finish, that can be made into extremely useful costume props that will stand up to pretty close viewing by refinishing, i.e. by plating them.

Electroplating a Cheap Ring

One such ring was bought for pennies with a view to upgrading it. As supplied, it looked pretty cheap. It was stamped as 925 (silver), but certainly wasn't!

ORDER OF WORK

1. The first job was to gently ease one claw of the setting, then another, just enough to release the (glass) stone, which was put to one side. The ring had a varnish or lacquer coating, which was then thoroughly cleaned off with a glass-fibre pen to get down to the metal and make sure no varnish remained. When it was completely clean, it was set up for copper-plating.

2. Electroplating can be done at a very simple level. The equipment needed is a power supply, a container with your plating solution (for copper, a solution of copper sulphate and sulphuric acid), an anode plate of copper in your solution connected to the + of the power supply, and the workpiece to be plated (the ring, in this instance) on a piece of wire as the cathode connected to the – of the power supply.

Fig. 5.83 The ring had a good look to it from a distance.

Fig. 5.84 Unfortunately, this ring wouldn't be easy to resize.

Fig. 5.85 Ring with the 'stone' removed.

3. In simple terms, with the system arranged as described, and the voltage set to about 1.2V, with the ring suspended in the solution, it takes around three minutes to copper-plate the ring, giving a nice bright, shiny ring shank.

4. You may choose to leave the ring copper-plated. You will need to polish the ring, place the stone back in and gently ease the setting claws back in place. Copper-plating looks fine when polished, giving a 'rose gold' colour, though if left would need regular polishing, as it does tend to go a very unrealistic colour very quickly. To further improve it, it will need to be gold-plated.

5. Check the ring for coverage, clean and burnish so it is nice and smooth for the gold-plating process. It is well worth making sure the copper-plating is good and successful before wasting gold solution on plating a questionable job.

6. The little tank is thoroughly cleaned in the changeover from copper to gold, and instead of using copper anodes, we use the single graphite block as an anode. The technique is the same, but our gold solution plates at around 4.7V.

7. After plating, the ring was thoroughly washed and very lightly polished to look like the real gold that it is.

Fig. 5.86 The plating works better if the copper is in good contact with the ring.

Fig. 5.87 Rig up a support (not metal).

Fig. 5.88 The copper-plated ring.

Fig. 5.89 Place the stone back in the setting.

Fig. 5.90 Gently ease the claws back in place.

Fig. 5.91 The ring polished up.

Fig. 5.92 The copper-plated ring could work for a more 'rustic' look.

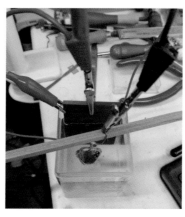

Fig. 5.93 The ring being gold-plated.

Fig. 5.94 Move the ring to make sure of even coverage.

Fig. 5.95 The gold-plated ring, polished and looking much more expensive than the original piece.

Fig. 5.96 The rings straight from the 3D printer.

Fig. 5.97 Ring with most of the support structure removed.

Electroplating a Printed Ring

A leaf ring was printed in resin, purely as a test-piece to demonstrate how it is possible to ultimately gold-plate plastic.

ORDER OF WORK

1. The ring was printed in an ABS-like resin on a Mars 2 Pro printer, at 20 microns definition. After all supports were removed, the ring was brush painted with conductive graphite paint (from Cat Music).
2. Once it was completely dry, it was briskly brushed with a stiff nylon brush to remove all excess paint, leaving only a thin layer of the graphite (all that is needed to conduct the electricity). Any excess paint will form a crust that can break away later with your precious plating. This should now look just like pencil lead in colour (see Fig. 5.98).
3. The graphite-coated ring was then suspended in the copper solution on a piece of wire as a cathode, and plated – rotating it every 20s or so in the wire to ensure an even coverage. At about 1.2V, it should come out lovely and shiny. If the voltage is too high and it plates too fast, it will go red, dark and matt.

Fig. 5.98 After the carbon solution has been applied and dried.

Fig. 5.99 The volts will fluctuate slightly.

Fig. 5.100 Straight from the solution.

Fig. 5.101 Polished up.

Fig. 5.102 A copper-plated leaf.

4. Once fully coated, everything was cleaned and the tank changed for gold-plating (you need to plate gold on top of copper) and then the plastic ring was gold-plated.

It works – though a plastic ring that bends will cause the plating to come away. The value of the technique will be that a brooch, badge or heaven knows what can be made in almost any material, and using this technique of graphite coating, can then be copper-plated, followed by silver- or gold-plating. A further example of this is a little electroformed ivy leaf. This is a real leaf that has been painted in graphite, and then copper-plated to a much greater thickness, so that it is self-supporting (using the same equipment). Leaves, lace-work and many other delicate things may be coated and formed in this way. They can then be further plated in silver or gold.

6
BAGS, POUCHES AND POCKETS

INTRODUCTION AND HISTORY

Bags are essentially transporters for anything that you want to keep with you on a journey or while working or gaming. They also protect the contents and are used to identify and organize. Of course, bags and pouches are used all over the world and can be made of any fabric that is readily available in the area. They have a very practical use and can be extremely plain, made of any strong, pliable material and closed and carried in a very rudimentary way. The pouch may be closed with a drawstring and either hung from the waist or over an arm. However, as with all costume accessories, they have also been used to show the wealth, style or power of the owner and became fashion items.

Many bags with ancient histories have been redesigned to suit the contemporary trends. The satchel, for instance, was used by Roman soldiers and monks, BC300–400, then becoming fashionable in the seventeenth century, adopted by the military and used universally by schoolchildren from the 1950s onwards into the twenty-first century, where it has become an expensive, genderless fashion bag.

Medieval and Before

Leather was often fashioned into a bag and used to carry currency of any type, be it coins, gold or jewellery. These pouches could be in the form of a circle, pulled up with a drawstring, or a bag made from two or more parts, as shown in Fig. 6.1.

Bags were originally created out of necessity, but often used to portray a message. Many of the examples that have survived are of a religious nature and there are also many examples in manuscripts, illuminations, sculptures and tapestries. As early as the fifth century, we can see pouches hanging from the waist of wealthy men and women,

Fig. 6.1 Showing the different styles of drawstring bags.

Fig. 6.2 A bicolour and a velvet medieval-type pouch (from the RADA archives).

often made from the same material as their skirts or breeches, and decorated with religious or family designs. They could be simple envelope bags with loops to attach it to a belt, or have many pockets and elaborate metal flaps. Although pockets, as we know them today, were rare, parts of the clothes were used to carry personal items, such as the liripipe of the hats and the bagpipe sleeves. The Scottish sporran, made from leather or skin, was certainly around in the twelfth century.

By the fifteenth century, there are many examples found of structured bags with complicated iron clasps depicting cathedrals and churches. The bags were often made of leather, silk or velvet and had complicated closing mechanisms.

Sixteenth Century

The fifteenth and sixteenth centuries saw the Renaissance in full swing, and the art and fashion influenced bag design. You see bags and purses made of leather or silk, often embroidered and either drawn together at the top, closed with a flap or attached to a steel frame.

The bags hanging from the waist became more complicated in design, sometimes with multiple pockets on the front and inner pockets.

Sweet (swete) bags were seen for the first time; these were small pouches containing herbs and spices to counter the environmental smells of the time. The sixteenth century saw bags being used by both men and women. Large satchels made from leather or heavy jute or linen cloth were worn across the body by travellers and workers.

As the fashions in skirts and breeches became more full around the hips, the smaller pouches were hung from the waist within the garments, accessed through slits in the seams forming an early type of pocket.

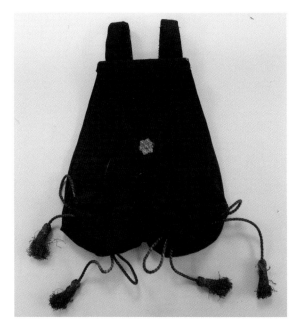

Fig. 6.3 The bags became quite complicated patterns (from the RADA archives).

Fig. 6.4 The bag has smaller drawstring bags on the front.

Fig. 6.5 Jewelled metal frames were common place (from the RADA archives).

Seventeenth Century

Bags were still being hung from the waist; however, the 'pockets' from the previous century remained, as the breeches became slim and pockets became part of the design.

When frockcoats became fashionable in the second half of the century, pockets became an integral part of the design and remained in the design of jackets and waistcoats for men to the present day. Women's pockets became flat pouches that hung from the waist under their skirts. Although not seen, these bags were highly embroidered and were worn well into the following century.

There were also many different forms of bags coming into fashion. Gaming bags were often used during gambling games; these were heavily embroidered, often with gold-work renderings of family crests or religious decorations. There were drawstring bags with a solid bottom for keeping your gambling 'pot' safely on the table. Sweet bags were still in use and knotting also became a popular form of bag manufacture towards the end of the century. The metal clasp we associate with evening bags today was in use in this century. Many bags were flat, heavily embroidered pouches, either clasped or closed with a drawstring; they became increasingly complex in design and many of the surviving examples were made of tapestry.

Eighteenth Century

Knotted tobacco pouches were reassigned to carry coins. These were long tubes, closed at either end with a slit down one side and rings that were pushed towards the ends to close the pouch. Tobacco pouches or 'wallets' could also be knitted or crocheted and were often intricately beaded.

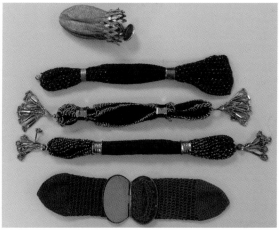

Fig. 6.6 The rings on the pouches held the coins in place.

Although pockets were still being hung beneath the skirts, pretty drawstring bags hung from the wrist also became popular. These could be embroidered with gold-work, thread or ribbon, they could be beaded or made of chain mail. These bags were also made into framed bags, the clasps being made of tortoiseshell, ivory and horn, wood and metal, including zinc and copper.

Gaming bags were still popular in the eighteenth century and bags, generally, were being used increasingly for larger items. Work bags kept any sewing, knitting, crocheting or knotting work and were also often highly embroidered.

Pocket books also became popular, being an early form of Filofax, containing letters, cards, diaries, handkerchiefs and other small, flat items.

Reticule is the term often used for bags from the end of the eighteenth century. The neo-classical ladies' fashions of the time were sheer and close-fitting and made the carrying of bags essential. The name may have come from the French for ridiculous (the media thinking they look comical), or from the Latin 'reticulum' meaning net. They were also called 'indispensables'.

Nineteenth Century

In the nineteenth century, bags of all sizes were popular as both a fashion item and practical tool. Although there were many professional bag-makers in the previous centuries, ladies' handbags were first commercially manufactured in 1885. This meant that ranges of handbags, often leather, were produced more affordably.

The Gladstone bag was made popular by William Ewart Gladstone who was Prime Minister four times between 1864 and 1898. The bag had a solid bottom and a solid clasp that kept the bag square, protecting its contents; it had many 'shelves' and pockets. For this reason, it

Fig. 6.8 A close-up of the beaded bag in Fig. 6.7.

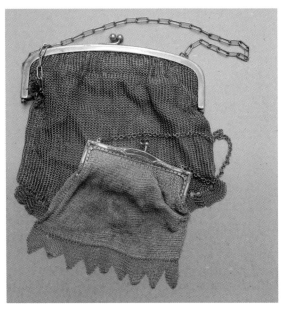

Fig. 6.9 Chain-mail bags with tiny links
(from the RADA archives).

Fig. 6.7 Tiny beads of glass and metal made up the bags.

was taken up by doctors who had started visiting their patients and so had to take many of their medicines with them.

Ladies also made their own bags or had them made bespoke. These were knotted, embroidered, mailled, knitted, beaded, painted or carved and, although at times, closed with a drawstring, had elaborate silver clasps with jewelled closures and silk linings. Clasps on many expensive bags were made from silver. Ivory was still popular, though an increasing distaste for it encouraged the invention by American John Hyatt of celluloid, which was developed from collodion. Celluloid could be moulded into intricate shapes and designs. Although beset with manufacturing problems (mostly due to the highly volatile nature of celluloid), these were popular until the invention of plastics in the early twentieth century.

As explored in the previous chapter, chatelaines were also a popular way of carrying tools such as keys, sewing items, dance cards and glasses. They consisted of a hook that clasped on to the waist and hung items from chains or ribbons. Used by all classes, being ever more ornate with wealth, these were employed throughout the world in different forms.

Carpet bags, so often mentioned in Victorian-based scripts, started life as merely rolling your possessions in a carpet to travel; this was cleverly folded on to a stake to form a handle. During Victorian times, these were redesigned to form a permanent bag, traditionally made from Brussels' carpet and used to carry luggage, as people were travelling more with the invention of the railways.

Dorothy bags were penned, these being drawstring bags, often made in the fabric of the dress worn and popularized in 1880 by a play of the same name.

Twentieth Century

The twentieth century saw the invention of plastics, the discovery of aluminium, and colour co-ordination and 'designer' bags.

In the early part of the century, the term 'handbag', previously assigned to men, was taken as an alternative term for the reticule. Bags began the century small, often with clasps of silver or gun metal, but as women became more active, both in exercise and work, they became bigger. By 1910, the fashion was for bags 30cm square. Smaller bags were still used for evening events; these could be Dorothy bags or framed, often with chain handles. All the materials over the centuries were used during this century: chain mail, leather, tapestry, beading and all forms of embroidery.

Leather was increasingly being used and was dyed many colours, though during and after the First World War, the colours were limited to black, brown or navy due to the limitations of supply. There were also exotic leathers, such as crocodile and snakeskin among the rich.

In the 1920s, the invention of plastic resulted in many more varied clasps, both in colour and design. It made bags very much cheaper and many novelty bags were made in the shape of animals or fruit. However, the clutch bag (or 'pochette') was also popularized in the 1920s. Often made of leather or silk, it sometimes had a thumb or handstrap on the back to allow the hand to be free when required.

By 1935, it became fashionable to match your shoes, handbags and often hats and gloves; this was enabled by a council being set up to standardize the colours being produced. Highly glamourized designer bags were created, such as the 'sac a depeches' designed by Buggatti for Hermes and later renamed the 'Kelly bag' after Grace Kelly.

The Second World War brought shortages again, though the practicalities of war popularized the shoulder bag for a short while. Many people

Fig. 6.10 Small bag c. 1950.

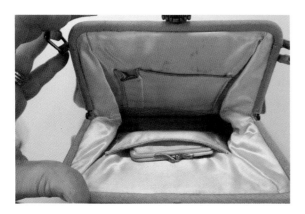

Fig. 6.11 Showing the inside of the 1950s bag, beautifully lined.

Fig. 6.12 Embroidered bags were also fashionable in the 1950s.

would knot themselves a shopping bag; these bags were often also crocheted. This was followed by a huge range of small bags. The bucket bags of the war years (used to carry gas masks) became smaller and framed bags were back throughout the 1940s and 1950s.

Although fake leather had been invented in the nineteenth century, the shortage and subsequent tax on leather encouraged the production of 'vynide' and many bags from this day forward would be made with fake (faux or vegan) leather.

The 1960s brought, again, many plastic novelty bags, but also larger, multi-pocketed bags with both hand- and shoulder-straps. Duffel bags and multi-buckled bags were made to match the fashions of the music or culture of the time. The 1970s brought a more 'homemade' look to the bags, with crochet, straw and patchwork often being seen.

Towards the end of the century, personal bags became smaller again, with the cross-the-body bags and 'bum bags' of the 1990s, and wheeled suitcases becoming more practical for travel.

PROJECT 1 BEADED BAG

Materials Required

- A large beading frame with capacity for at least 68 warp threads
- 50m beading thread (this should be able to pass through the bead three times)
- Long beading needles
- Approximately 10,000 2mm seed beads, 1mm hole, purple
- Approximately 300 each of dark red, pink, red, dark green, mid-green and pale green
- A few brown, yellow and orange for centre of flowers
- A large-holed bead for the top of the tassel
- A means of melting or gluing thread ends (a lighter or heating tool can be used for this; alternatively, jewellers' glue may be used)

Order of Work

THREADING UP

1. Cut 13, 1m-long threads and fold in half. Knot the ends to form a 4cm-long loop.
2. Place the knot over the centre pick at the top end of the loom and pull down to the lower wooden rod, passing the threads through the separator top and bottom.

3. Knot the threads together and loop over the centre pick on the lower rod.
4. Repeat the process with ten folded lengths on one side and eleven on the other, forming sixty-eight warp threads in all. When knotting the lower threads, try to ensure the knot is at an equal distance from the pick.
5. Loosen the rods at either end and twist them until the threads are under tension.
6. Keep the length of the warp threads along the bottom; they will be needed to complete the bag.

> **NOTE**
>
> If you haven't quite got the knots in the same place, some of the threads may be looser than others. In this case, a folded piece of card can be pushed between the rod and the threads to bring those into line.

THREADING THE BEADS

For this method, you are required to have many threads threaded up before weaving. There are rotating bowls specifically designed for this, though I have found that filling a bowl with beads and then thrusting a long, threaded beading needle into the bowl repeatedly is very effective. The threaded beads are shown in Figs 6.13 and 6.14.

Fig. 6.13 The loose beads.

Fig. 6.14 Threaded up.

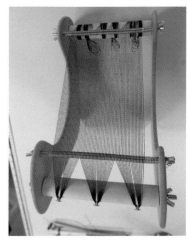

Fig. 6.15 The weaving loom threaded up.

WEAVING WITH ONE COLOUR

When beading with no pattern, it is easier and quicker to used two weft threads: one to hold the beads and one to pass over the top side of the weft threads to hold it securely.

1. Cut a long piece of thread and fill most of the thread with beads. Leave a good amount at the end for expansion when weaving.
2. Knot the start of the thread to one end warp thread at the top of the work.
3. Cut another long thread and knot to the opposite end warp thread at the same height.
4. Offer the beads to the underside of the warp threads, making sure there is only one bead between each warp thread.

> **NOTE**
>
> If the warp threads are the right distance apart, the beads should sit between the threads neatly. The thread spacing can be altered slightly by tightening or releasing the screw on the end of the spacing spring.

5. Take the beaded long thread through the beads from the front side of the weft threads, so securing them in place.
6. Repeat this operation, until the required length of weaving is achieved.
7. After each row, you may pull on the two threads until the beads are sitting tightly, but be beware of pulling them too tightly as this will reduce the drapability of the piece.

WEAVING A DESIGN

Always work from a pattern and mark off the rows as you go.

8. Count the number of each coloured bead required and thread them on to the beading thread, as shown in Fig. 6.17.
9. Offer it up to the warp threads from below, as before, to make sure you have the required beads.
10. Thread the beads on to the thread and push through between the warp threads from the back.

Fig. 6.16 Pass the beads under and through the warp threads, one through each gap.

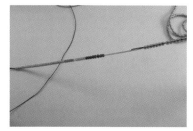

Fig. 6.17 Count the beads on to the needle, using the pattern as a guide.

Fig. 6.18 The pattern starts to take shape.

Fig. 6.19 Take care to fill each gap between the threads.

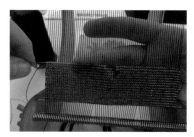

Fig. 6.20 Push the beads forward through the warp threads to help get the needle through.

Fig. 6.21 Take care to thread all the beads from behind.

11. Using the same thread, go round the last warp thread and pass it through the beads from the front side of the warp threads as before and pull through.
12. Move on to the next line of the pattern and repeat until the pattern is completed.

ADDING IN MORE THREAD

13. When you run out of thread, leave enough to weave back into the work.
14. Pass the thread through the beads of the row above the one just worked, along the opposite side of the warp threads and pull out to the back.
15. Weave the new thread from the same point but in the row below, out to the end and continue the work. This is because the holes in the beads may be too small to allow too many threads to pass through them and it also allows for these two threads to be knotted together for extra security.

> **NOTE**
>
> If the threads are synthetic or silk, the threads may be melted together with a small flame or heating tool, as shown in Fig. 6.27.

THE BOTTOM CURVE

There are a few ways of finishing woven beadwork. They usually consist of knotting off the finished rows or/and weaving the threads back into the work.

In this example, the warp threads were redirected into weft threads by taking them through the work when they were finished with. This helps the integrity of the bag. There will still be some threads to be knotted; when there are, keep some of the spare thread, which can be left inside the bag when sewn together.

16. Following the pattern, as you finish each row, knot with the weaving thread and pass through the remaining beads.

17. Continue until you reach the end of the pattern.
18. Bring all the remaining threads to the point of the bag and secure with buttonhole stitch.

> **NOTE**
>
> Doing this will necessitate undoing the warp threads from the frame. To maintain tension, I found adding a washer on to the side wing nut and winding them round kept them sufficiently tight for the short time required, as shown in Fig. 6.23.

ATTACHING THE BACK TO THE FRONT

If you were to just sew the back to the front (which is an option), you would inevitably have the colour of the threads showing through. To avoid this, weaving in an extra bead is a better option.

19. Take a piece of the thread and tie off at the top of the pieces.
20. Take the thread though three to four beads on the upper side of the back.
21. Add a bead on and weave the thread through two to four beads on the other side.
22. Continue this on the bottom of the piece.
23. Vary the number of beads you weave in, to avoid creating a pulled space down the length.
24. Repeat on the other side of the work.
25. Ensure that the thread remains on the top side of the fabric, so that the beads can lie together well.

THE TOP, HONEYCOMB SECTION

26. Undo the knots at the top end of the warp threads and cut the loops.
27. Knot two threads together, miss two threads.
28. Continue this until you have gone round the top of the bag.

You can proceed either by completing one row at a time or several rows as you go. To work a few columns at a time:

Fig. 6.22 The finished pattern can be rolled around the frame.

Fig. 6.23 Holding the tension with the wing nuts at the side.

Fig. 6.24 Beginning to shape the bottom of the bag.

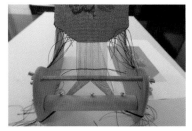

Fig. 6.25 Carry on, keeping the tension tight.

Fig. 6.26 One side completed.

Fig. 6.27 Melting some loose threads with a hot gun.

Fig. 6.28 Taking the excess threads to the bottom of the bag.

Fig. 6.29 The threads in place to make the tassel.

Fig. 6.30 Both sides completed.

Fig. 6.31 Joining the two sides together, incorporating an extra bead.

Fig. 6.32 Continue down, making sure you vary the number of beads taken each side.

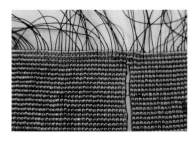

Fig. 6.33 Showing the 'seamless' seam.

Fig. 6.34 The bottom of the bag will look like this.

Fig. 6.35 Thread each alternate warp thread.

Fig. 6.36 Create the honeycomb.

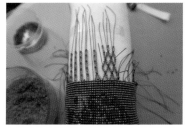

Fig. 6.37 Continuing the honeycomb.

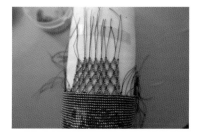

Fig. 6.38 The honeycomb should look like this.

Fig. 6.39 Hold the loose threads with double-sided tape.

Fig. 6.40, Fig. 6.41 and Fig. 6.42 The formation of the top of the tassel.

29. Take the left thread from each of the remaining threads and thread them (two purple, one green, one red) and repeat four times.
30. Carry out an even number of these, as shown in Fig. 6.35.
31. Secure these threads to some double-sided tape as you work.
32. Take each right warp thread, thread (two purple and one green) and then take the thread through the red one on the row next to it. Repeat this until you reach to top red. Secure the thread.
33. Wait until you have done a few columns before finishing off.

34. To finish off, thread five purple beads to the left of a pair of warp threads. Take the right warp thread from the pair to the left and pass this through the same five beads in the opposite direction.
35. Knot the threads to the next shell created to secure.
36. Either melt or glue the knot with jewellers' glue.

MAKING THE TASSEL

1. Pass the threads through your larger bead, leaving twelve threads free round the edge.

2. Thread enough beads on each of these threads to cover the large bead.
3. Tie in pairs.
4. Secure the beads by taking a thread round under the large beads and tying off.

LINING THE BAG

5. Cut the pieces from the pattern and sew using French seams.
6. Sew a tuck into the top in the marked position so that the tuck faces into the bag.
7. Open up the seams on each side of the tuck and create an opening. Neaten with button-hole stitch.
8. Stitch as marked to the beadline below the honeycomb.
9. Turn over the top and stitch to the top red beads, incorporating any thread ends as you go.
10. Add a ribbon to form an opening and handle.

Fig. 6.43 Create a pattern for the lining and French seam the outside of the bag.

Fig. 6.44 Stitching the lining in place.

Fig. 6.45 The finished bag.

Fig. 6.46 Creating the inside opening.

PROJECT 2 CHAIN-MAIL BAG

The chain-mail bag has been used throughout recorded history. They can be lined or left as they are. They can be made from many different metals, though steel ones will have a tendency to rust. Stainless steel is a good option for the earlier bags, though they can be expensive and much harder to work with; however, they have an authentic look and are very strong. The later bags were often silver or silver-plate, so it would depend on your budget which one you use.

For this bag, I am using silver-plated steel rings, half of them are closed, half open. Plated rings are often copper-based, but the steel makes the rings quite strong, so there is not the necessity to solder them shut, and if the plate comes off, the steel won't jar on the eye. You do have to look after it though to prevent rust in the long term. Solid-silver rings would be ideal, though they are more expensive and very soft, so requiring soldering closed.

All the instructions are assuming you are using both closed and open rings. If possible, get saw-cut rings, as these have sharper edges and close much more effectively.

Materials Required

- 1000 6mm diameter, 1mm wire thickness silver-plated steel rings, open
- 1000 6mm diameter, 1mm wire thickness silver-plated steel rings, closed
- 11cm bag clasp
- Nitromors (optional)
- Silver-plating solution
- Ten small steel beads for decoration
- Two smooth-face pliers

Order of Work

The beginning of chain mail is always the trickiest, as the rings never seem to sit in the correct

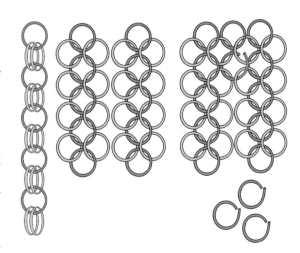

Fig. 6.47 Showing the build-up of the chain mail.

positions for long; once you get going, it does become easier. You can either work horizontally or vertically. Here, we use both methods, first, vertically.

1. Take one open ring, add four closed rings and close the ring.
2. Put another ring through two of these rings and add two more closed rings before closing the ring.
3. Continue (2) thirteen times. You will have a chain of rings, two and then one formation (shown in Fig. 6.48).
4. Lay out the chain as shown in Fig. 6.49, so that the links lie flat.
5. At this point, you could do each line separately, as shown later, though I find it quicker to get the chains stable by making another chain in the same way. First, make another chain in the same way.
6. Lay both chains on a piece of masking tape, so that the single rings sit beneath each other, as shown in Fig. 6.50.
7. Join the chains, by adding a ring to the four rings surrounding the single ring on both chains, using the tape to keep the chains in position.
8. The chain mail should now start becoming more stable and you can add more loops to it.

Fig. 6.48 Chain formation of two chains in one.

Fig. 6.49 Showing how to lay the chain.

Fig. 6.50 Make sure you lay both chains in the same direction.

Fig. 6.51, Fig. 6.52, and Fig. 6.53 Showing the building of the chain mail.

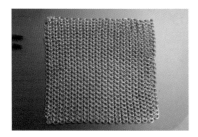

Fig. 6.54 Showing the building of the chain mail.

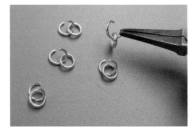

Fig. 6.55 Keep a number of links open for ease of working.

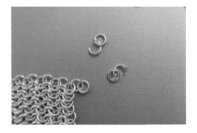

Fig. 6.56 Start a vertical row with two links and lay them in the same direction as previous rows.

Fig. 6.57 Add two more links, ensuring that the previous finished links contain four rings.

Fig 6.58 Both sides made, ready to fold over.

Fig 6.59 I used a tailor's ham to pin the bag for joining.

9. Take an open ring, add two closed rings and take the ring through the first two loops, following the pattern of the other rings. Then take an open ring and add one closed ring and add it to the following two rings on the row, as shown in Figs 6.51 to 6.54.

10. Continue to the end of the row.

11. Continue until you have achieved thirty rows.

> **TIP**
>
> I find it easier to have several open rings, with a closed ring added, ready, so that I can pick each one up without letting go of the chain mail work (Fig. 6.55).

12. You can now either make another square and join them together, or work sideways on this square and fold it over. Working sideways is shown in Figs 6.56–6.57.

13. Leave eight chains open down each side (or to match the number of holes you have in your clasp).

14. To join the pieces together, stabilize the chains with tape or pins, make sure the rings are facing the same direction on both edges and join the chains by placing the rings through four rings at a time.

15. There are several ways of closing the lower edge. I have chosen to join with rings through each chain. I then grouped these rings together in threes and joined with another chain, also adding a small bead on each chain to finish.

THE CLASPED FRAME

16. The clasp being used is a cheaply bought one and I would prefer it to look silver. To do this we will be using silver-plating liquid (also described in Workshop Tools and Equipment in the Introduction). This liquid is sold as a way of repairing silver-plated jewellery, but does a pretty good job of putting a very thin coat of plate on to other metals.

17. The cheaper metals tend to have a protective coating, which can prevent the plating

Fig. 6.60 Chainmaille bag with both sides joined.

Fig. 6.61 Bottom closed with added ball fringe.

Fig. 6.62 The clasp in its 'new' form.

Fig. 6.63 Applying the Nitromors.

Fig. 6.64 Removing the Nitromors.

Fig. 6.65 The first application of plating solution, which showed that the clasp needed some more rubbing down.

Fig. 6.66 Rubbing the clasp down more using a soft wire brush.

Fig. 6.67 Reapplying the solution.

Fig. 6.68 Polishing up the silver plate.

Fig. 6.69 The silver is gradually brought out.

Fig. 6.70 Attaching the bag to the clasp.

Fig. 6.71 The finished bag without a handle.

fluid from adhering, so the first thing to do is it get that off. Here I chose to use Nitromors – a paint-stripper. Make sure you protect your hands when using this, it is very strong. You can also use an abrasive material to rub the frame down in preparation. I also chose to rub it with a wire brush.

18. Apply the plating solution using a soft cloth – I am using a leather dye dauber here.
19. Then rub with a clean, soft cloth. If the silver doesn't develop, you may need to reapply the solution or rub down the metal further. It is worth the work as the results are excellent and a very cheap way of plating.
20. Attach the bag to the clasp using single rings in each hole provided.

THE HANDLE

The handle is made with a simple, plain chain, using 2 × 2 rings.

21. Loop one open ring through four closed rings and close the ring.
22. Add a second ring alongside the first joining (open) ring.
23. Pull out a pair of the closed rings.
24. Add two closed rings to another open ring.
25. Loop this new open ring through the pair of closed rings (23).
26. Add a second ring alongside this new joining ring (25) as in (22).
27. Repeat from (23) to (26) until the chain is the desired length.
28. Secure on to the clasp with two rings using the holes provided.

Fig. 6.72 Four rings into one.

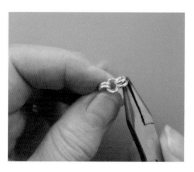

Fig. 6.73 Take two of the rings and add one ring.

Fig. 6.74 Before closing this ring, add another two rings.

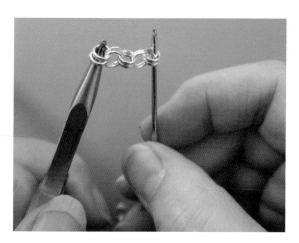

Fig. 6.75 Continue in this way until your handle is long enough.

Fig. 6.76 The finished bag.

PROJECT 3 THE EMBROIDERED BAG

Embroidery has been used throughout time to enhance soft furniture and clothing accessories. Embroidery takes time and, therefore, must either be worked on for many hours or be paid for, both of which shows that you are monied – either you have the time to sew or you have the money to pay someone else to do the work. Embroidery also has the added benefit of strengthening the fabric. Many costumes that have survived hundreds of years have done so because of the embroidery embellishments.

The bag in the example was particularly popular in the eighteenth century, though the techniques can be used on costume right back to medieval times. The bags were often lined with compartments or pockets and the inside was often embroidered as well.

Materials Required

- A clasp-frame in keeping with the period – in this case an imitation carved ivory, which was found second-hand on eBay
- Half a metre of outer linen fabric (if less is available, the pattern may be tacked on to a larger piece of cotton fabric to allow it to be placed in the embroidery frame)
- A small amount of finer fabric, for the lining
- An embroidery frame, large enough to accommodate the whole of the embroidery pattern
- Paper, pencil and ruler for drawing the pattern
- A transfer pencil or heat-erasing pen for transferring the pattern to the fabric
- Embroidery needles
- Assorted embroidery thread
- Small amount of iron-on interfacing

The Pattern

1. Place the clasp on a piece of paper, making sure that the paper is long enough to accommodate the length of the bag (Fig. 6.77).
2. Draw straight down from the edges of the clasp and across the bottom, showing the approximate length and width of the bag.
3. Remove the clasp and divide the pattern into four equal pieces (Fig. 6.78).
4. Splay out the pattern at the bottom; this has the effect of giving a bit of room at the bottom of the bag and straightening the top of the pattern to enable the sides of the bag to sit out, giving more room inside (Fig. 6.79).
5. Curve the sides of the bag to give a more sympathetic shape to the bag.
6. Design and draw a pattern to fit the bag side. I have included the one used here, which can be adapted or completely redrawn to your own design.

Fig. 6.77 I found this 'ivory-looking' clasp on eBay, a style that was very popular for bags from the eighteenth century onwards.

Fig. 6.78 and Fig. 6.79 You can make the bag any shape you would like.

Order of Work

1. Take the main fabric and iron some interfacing on to the back where the embroidery is to be, to give stability to the stitching. (Do not cut the pattern out as the fabric needs to be large enough to fit the embroidery frame.)
2. Transfer the pattern of the embroidery on to the main fabric using tailoring carbon paper, transfer paper, water-soluble pen or heat-erasing pen. Fig. 6.80 shows the pattern being transferred using a heat-erasing pen and a light box.
3. Place the fabric in the embroidery frame, keeping the fabric tight.
4. Gather together the materials you need, as shown in Fig. 6.81.
5. Carry out the embroidery. If you have appliquéd sections, do these first and then build the embroidery around it. The appliqué pieces can be worked on separately, as shown in the pictures, and then slip-stitched on to the piece.

> **TIP**
>
> If you are using a new frame, it is a good idea to wrap both the inner and outer loop with tape (I find bias binding good for this). Make sure the tape is evenly wound, it allows for a tighter fit and less fabric slippage.

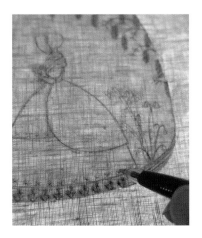

Fig. 6.80 A light-box is a useful tool to transfer patterns.

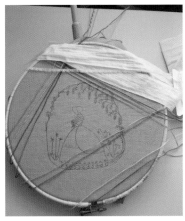

Fig. 6.81 Collecting together the tools and seeing the colours together.

Fig. 6.82 Building the skirt using appliqué. Using a cardboard template, fold and press the main ribbon round the pattern, remove the cardboard and then slip-stitch to the linen chosen for the bag.

Fig. 6.83 Flowers were embroidered on the skirt using straight-stitch and French knots. Then cut the overskirt in cardboard and press the pink silk ribbon round the template. It might be best to put a small piece of interfacing to the back of this to support the stitching.

Fig. 6.84 Threads were stitched every 5mm round the overskirt, then buttonhole stitched to form 'loops'.

Fig. 6.85 Folds were embroidered using stem-stitch and more flowers were added using straight-stitches and French knots.

APPLIQUÉ

When appliquéing a piece, it is best to use a fine fabric that irons well. First, make a template in cardboard and iron the fabric round the cardboard. If it does not stay, either use another fabric or tack the under-wrap in place, then carry out any embroidery or edging and then slip-stitch it in place.

6. Complete the embroidery to your taste. I have included some useful embroidery stitches but there are many ways to build the picture.
7. Cut around the embroidery using the pattern (don't forget to include seam allowances).
8. Also, cut a pattern out for the back of the bag and two pieces for the lining. If you are going to include an inside pocket, cut this out also.

Fig. 6.86 The overskirt was then stitched in place.

Fig. 6.87 The yellow flowers were sewn using stem-stitch and basket-stitch.

Fig. 6.88 The blue flowers were stitched using straight-stitch throughout.

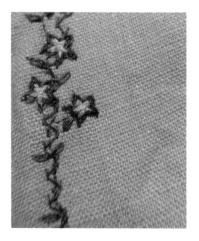

Fig. 6.89 The clematis flowers were stitched using satin stitch.

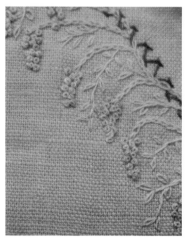

Fig. 6.90 The wisteria was formed using chain-stitch and French knots.

Fig. 6.91 The lady's bonnet was appliquéd on after a small piece of lace was attached and embellished with ladder-stitch, French knots for hair and flowers with a lace shawl and French knot appliquéd sleeves and satin-stitched arms.

9. Take the pocket, if required, embroider and attach it to the right side of the lining fabric.
10. Sew the outside seams of the main and lining fabric.
11. Turn the lining inside out and, placing the right side of the main fabric and the lining, stitch round all edges, leaving a small gap for turning through.
12. Turn through to the right side and slip-stitch the gap.
13. Stitch the purse to the clasp. Most clasps have holes in to stitch the bag to. However, some have a double skin, which needs pinching together with pliers, and others will require gluing.
14. Carry out any further embellishments, such as some embroidery or ribbon, to cover up the stitching of the bag to the clasp.

Fig. 6.92 The ground was formed by stitching two rows of running stitches and running a thread from one line to the other and grass added with stem-stitch and French knot daisies.

Fig. 6.93 The finished embroidery.

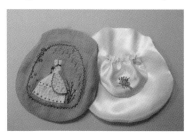

Fig. 6.95 Add the inside pocket before putting the bags together.

Fig. 6.94 Get the rest of the materials together and cut out.

Fig. 6.96 Complete the bag before sewing to the clasp.

Fig. 6.97 The finished bag showing the lining in place.

Fig. 6.98 The finished bag.

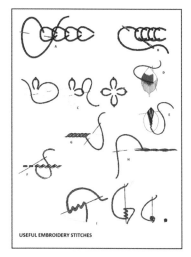

USEFUL EMBROIDERY STITCHES

7
SPECTACLES AND EYEGLASSES

INTRODUCTION AND HISTORY

Spectacles refer to two lenses that are fitted in front of the eyes through which to see, while an eyeglass refers to a single lens, very often held in front of the eyes. Of course, most people refer to all spectacles as 'glasses'.

There are many theories exploring who actually invented spectacles, Friar Roger Bacon and Salvino d'Armato of Florence being top of the list. The truth is likely to be that the natural progression of invention from research happened all around the world. In 1268, Roger Bacon wrote of the weaknesses of older eyes that could be helped with optical lenses, and the first recorded spectacles were in Pisa in 1286.

Medieval and Before

The earliest spectacles consisted of two magnifying glasses, riveted together, the lenses being made from ground quartz or 'beryl' (Berillus), and the frames of wood, leather or horn. The style is not unlike Fig. 7.1, though this is a later reincarnation in steel.

The fourteenth century saw a huge increase in the manufacture of spectacles. By the earlier fifteenth century, gold frames were being worn.

The spread of spectacles was accelerated by the invention of the Gutenberg Printing Press in 1450 and by the 1460s, Florence was producing large quantities of both convex and concave glasses, in graduated strengths.

Sixteenth Century

The main suppliers to Britain were the Dutch. Then mass-production techniques were invested in around Nuremburg, making lenses from grinding sheet glass, which reduced the quality.

Concave lenses were more commonly used and we see oval frames for the first time, though they were not common until the eighteenth century.

Many inventive ways of keeping the lenses in front of the eyes were seen, including tying round the head, attaching to the hat and ties around the ears.

Seventeenth Century

A further large increase in demand for spectacles came when the first newspaper appeared in 1665. More people needed to see to read.

Tinted glasses first became popular.

In 1675, split-bridge spectacles were seen. These were made of horn and had the bridge split lengthwise, which became a spring between the lens' frames as a method of keeping the spectacles on the nose.

The first metal-framed glasses came at the beginning of the century, though they were rare.

London formed its own city guild of spectacle-makers in 1629, increasing Britain's presence in the world trade.

PERSPECTIVE GLASSES
This was a single lens, usually with a handle with a hole to enable it to be hung round the neck and

held up to the eye when needing to see something close up.

PROSPECT GLASSES

Galileo popularized the telescope, closely followed by the binoculars. These were popular in the seventeenth century as spyglasses and sometimes were attached to sticks. The French called these lorgnettes, not to be confused with the lorgnettes associated with the eighteenth century, which were essentially eyeglasses on a stick handle.

Fig. 7.1 A riveted pair of spectacles.

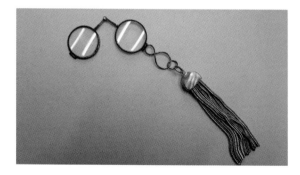

Fig. 7.2 The riveted spectacles being used as a lorgnette.

Fig. 7.3 An early twentieth-century lorgnette.

Fig. 7.4 A jewelled, folding lorgnette with case.

Eighteenth Century

In the 1720s, we see for the first time spectacles with arms. They did not reach the ears at first, intending only to grip on to the temples, with large rings on the end of the arms. These might have been made of steel and couldn't have been very comfortable.

Experiment in focusing discovered that reducing the aperture of the frames further enhanced the eyesight. This was the intension of glasses called 'Martin's Margins' (named after the inventor, Benjamin Margin), where a ring of horn would draw the eye to the centre of the frame.

Benjamin Franklin ordered a pair of spectacles in the 1760s, which had his two prescriptions split equally between the top and bottom of the lens, so inventing the bifocals, though these did not become commonplace until the nineteenth century.

Spectacles were not deemed very fashionable, which brought down the cost and at the same time made them even less popular with the rich, except during the time of lavishness from the middle of the century when hand-held glasses were developed into expensive, ornate statements of wealth. However, during this century, the arms of the spectacles finally reached the ears, albeit with a hinged, rather than a shaped arm.

Fig. 7.5 An early example of steel spectacles with arms and side shades. Note the straight arms with loops at the end.

THE QUIZZING GLASS

This was a type of perspective glass, also known as a lanister, though the term 'quizzer' was often used in England. It was also sometimes called a 'monocle', referring to an armless lens.

LORGNETTES

These being a two-lens frame, supported by a handle, they were hugely popular with the rich and were decorated lavishly with gold, porcelain, enamels, carved wood and ivory. The lenses would usually fold into the handle and would be worn from the wrist or kept in a bag. Another form of the lorgnette were the scissor-glasses, where the handle came from the middle of the frames.

Forever more inventive ways of placing the lenses were shown off by the rich, including in a walking stick, hat or even the hairstyle of your wife.

Nineteenth Century

From 1812, frames of gold and silver were more common and astigmatism lenses came into being by the 1820s. Tortoiseshell was also popularly used to make frames; this came from the hawksbill turtle.

After the lavishness of the eighteenth century, plain spectacles became more popular. Lorgnettes were still popular but a less decorative version,

often made from tortoiseshell or horn. In 1840, the pince-nez was reinvented and was popular until 1935.

The shape of the lenses varied through the century, going from large and round, to small and round, to small with various shapes, including oval, oblong, rectangle or hexagonal.

In the 1880s, we see the first purpose-made sunglasses, and the arms of the glasses were usually made to fit around the ears, though still in the hinged style. The arms still were finished with a loop for comfort, until the end of the century when we see arms curving around the ear. At this point, rolled gold and steel were being used to make the frames, which were very small. Ladies' glasses were especially small and delicate.

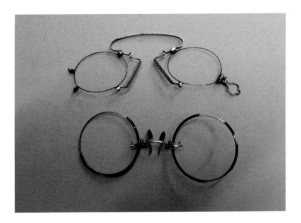

Fig. 7.6 Two examples of pince-nez, with a spring steel bridge and sprung clips.

Fig. 7.7 An early example of rimless glasses.

Fig. 7.8 Early twentieth-century faux tortoiseshell glasses.

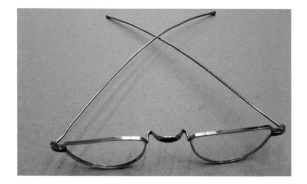

Fig. 7.9 Half-moon glasses – with straight arms.

THE MONOCLE

The monocle was a single-lensed frame with a double bridge on the back to allow the lens to be held by the muscles round the eye. Not everyone could wear one and they were required to be tailored to the size of the wearer's eye socket. They were not hugely popular, being brought back in the twentieth century as a more fashionable item.

CONTACT LENSES

The ability to manufacture glass contact lenses was possible for medical reasons from the 1880s, though this was not going to be popular, or affordable, until well into the twentieth century.

Twentieth Century

The look of glasses was little changed in the first part of the twentieth century, and the First World War required a practical solution to correcting eyesight. All the recent eye-pieces came into play: pince-nez, lorgnettes and monocles.

In the 1920s, the monocle became very popular as a fashion item and the spring-ended arms allowed the spectacles finally to sit on the ears comfortably. Frames became very small and delicate, sometimes rimless.

The 1930s brought purpose-made sunglasses, hugely popularized by Hollywood and the films now being seen, while the forties brought many plastic frames. A classic style was invented for men and women – the men's having a heavy straight top edge, while the women fashioned a slight 'cats-eye' appearance. Both these styles would be exaggerated during the 1950s. During the 1960s, the trendy frames for the young were heavy and small, though the earlier frames endured for the older generation. During the 1970 and 1980s, the frames became a lot larger; men would often wear metal-framed glasses again, while women wore frames sometimes extending out from their face.

Fig. 7.10 An example of mid-twentieth-century men's glasses – having returned many times in fashion as a style.

In the 1990s and into the next millennium, the frames became, once again, smaller and more practical and, although they have varied annually, this has remained the same.

CONTACT LENSES

Although lenses were available in the 1940s, they weren't really popular until the 1960s/1970s when new gas-permeable versions made them safer to wear. In the twenty-first century, they are commonplace and are often worn on stage with prop eyeglasses fitted with plain lenses when it is more practical to do so.

PROJECT 1 FOURTEENTH-CENTURY RIVETED SPECTACLES

The style of these spectacles is from the fourteenth century, when spectacles were becoming widely used. Generally, they were very simple affairs, consisting of a pair of lens-holders, each with an extension to reach over the nose and a rivet to hold the pair together. They could fold and open up, lightly gripping the bridge of the nose in most instances, or otherwise having to be held in place by hand. They often had little pin-holes in the lens-holders, which (just like a pin-hole camera) allowed the viewer to see in focus when the small hole was held close to the eye.

Lenses were glass by this time – an adaptation of the earlier rock-crystal magnifier, still rather crude, and intended for reading and writing, rather than distance correction.

There are several ways these can be made – by hand, using a fret saw to cut out the holders, by laser or by CNC mill.

In this period, glasses (or *occhiale* – meaning 'eyeglasses') were most commonly of wood, and we can use thin MDF sheet 1mm and 2mm thick. An appropriate coloured acrylic sheet may also be used. We would not advise using plywood or similar for this, as splintering is likely to occur, which would be very unpleasant near the face and hard to get a decent finish.

Materials Required

Prepare a full-size drawing and, if making by hand, copy, rough-cut out and stick to the sheet material with Pritt Stick or similar as a pattern to cut round.

The ideal (though long-winded) way is to make each lens-holder of three 1mm-thick layers or

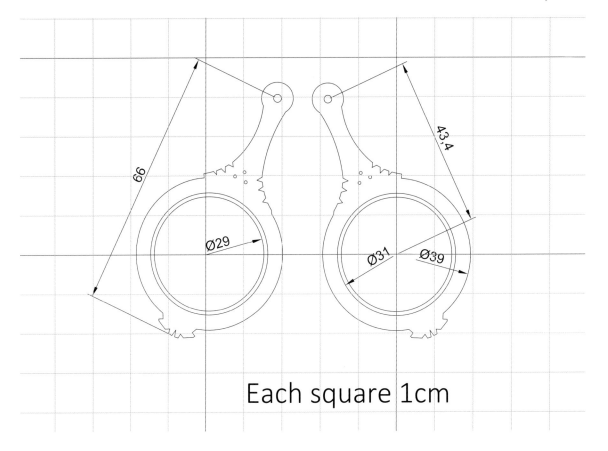

Each square 1cm

laminations, with the centre lamination having a slightly larger diameter hole in which the lens will sit. The two outer layers will have a slightly smaller hole, which will trap the lens, preventing it from falling out.

A slightly quicker way is to use one layer of 2mm, with a slightly larger internal diameter, which will house the lens, and one layer of 1mm with a slightly smaller internal diameter, which will be the front of the lens-holder, and glue the lens in from the back using epoxy adhesive.

Some glasses are ornamented with scribed detail. If you are doing this, it is best done now while still in the sheet. Some metal-working, marking-out tools are good for this, such as scribers and dividers. Once the lens hole is cut out, some markings will be much more difficult to make.

Order of Work

1. Drill a small hole (say 3mm diameter) in the middle of each lens area, thread the fret-saw blade through the hole and saw out each lens hole as cleanly and accurately as you can. Then clean up the resulting hole with half-round needle files or fine (600 grit) sandpaper.
2. Drill the end of the lens-holder for a small (2mm diameter) machine screw (bolt), which will pivot both holders together, forming the spectacles.
3. Cut out the outside shape of the lens-holder with the fret-saw, and clean up the edges with needle files and 600 grit sandpaper. The pin-holes can be drilled (about 1mm diameter) at this time.

4. Lenses should be cut with a saw (if 1mm acrylic), knife or scissors, if made from P.E.T., to the larger diameter, to be a snug fit in the frames. If the 2mm/1mm layering is being used, glue the two layers of MDF together with PVA, and allow to cure. If the 1mm/1mm/1mm layering is being used, glue one outer to the inner, allow to cure, insert the lens and make sure it is a good fit and the finish is good, and finally glue on the second outer to trap the lens – making sure you don't get excess glue on the lens.
5. If making these with a laser cutter, the 1mm/1mm/1mm is the method recommended, not forgetting to clean the edges before assembly. Scribed detail can, of course, be laser-etched as part of the cutting process. It is necessary to produce a drawing in CAD form for laser and any CNC processes, and requires the use of machines (albeit small ones) and associated software to do so. The advantage of this is accuracy and the ability to then produce as many as you like, very quickly, after you have done the initial leg-work. The cost of machines has come down phenomenally so they are affordable, and most of the software 'language' is fairly interchangeable – although there is a learning curve. The pair shown were made on the Stepcraft CNC router. These were of the 2mm/1mm layering but, in this instance, the 2mm layer was rebated by 1mm on the inside of the lens to accommodate the lens thickness (thus replicating the effect of the 1mm/1mm/1mm).

Fig. 7.11 Showing the cut-out shapes and holes drilled.

Fig. 7.12 Showing the inset and the cut-out acrylic sheet.

Fig. 7.13 Showing the cut ends.

6. Lenses were also profiled from 1mm acrylic on the CNC to fit the rebate in the 2mm MDF. Real glass should *not* be used. The real things had a rebate hand-carved into the thickness of the frame, and the lens was inserted by having a split in the rim, allowing it to open a little wider, which, once the lens was inserted, was usually held closed by wire wrapped around two lugs – one either side of the split. This is easily replicated by using fuse-wire or modelling wire.

7. Finishing may be varnish or painting to research or taste.

8. Finally, the two lens-holders should be joined together at the bridge by a 2mm nut and bolt with washer, filed flatter and smoothed, and tightened so as to be stiff but allow articulation.

A further perfectly viable method of making items such as these would be 3D printing (PLA for longevity). It is also possible to get 'wood' filament for these printers, which could look acceptable without painting.

Fig. 7.14 Showing the glazing.

Fig. 7.15 Showing the wired ends.

Fig. 7.16 Showing the rivet in place.

Fig. 7.17 The finished riveted spectacles.

PROJECT 2 LORGNETTE

This example is a replica of a tortoiseshell lorgnette of a fairly typical nineteenth-century style.

Materials Required

Acrylic sheet is available in a very large variety of colours and styles, and fortunately tortoiseshell is one of them, though not available in every thickness. A sheet of 3mm thick bronze tortoiseshell acrylic sheet was easily found and ordered on line, and the lorgnette and its components drawn up on a 2D CAD program.

This particular lorgnette was to be made with a desk-top CNC, such as are becoming more popular, but could also be made with modifications by CO_2 laser cutter, by band-saw and by hand tools. The CNC allows the spectacles to be rebated, which is not practical by other techniques (for further information please see Workshop Tools and Equipment in the Introduction).

The outline is drawn to the correct size, using researched photographs and available information. You will need to decide whether it will be made for left-hand or right-hand use, as the spectacles will need to be rebated at the back to accept the lenses.

Order of Work

1. Spectacles

Because the tortoiseshell acrylic is only available in limited thicknesses, it was decided to have the spectacles a total thickness of 3mm, and rebate the (1mm) lenses into that depth.

The specs are drawn, together with the rebate. All lines are 'welded' or 'joined' in the CAD program (so the outside shape of the spectacles becomes a single continuous line for the computer, not a series of separate lines, which would otherwise all be calculated separately).

When the CAD drawing (DWG or DXF) is imported into the CNC file, the rebate for the lenses is plotted first cutting at 1.7mm deep, followed by the internal cutting out for the lens cutting all the way through at 3mm and, finally, the outside profile that gives the actual spectacle shape, also at 3mm depth. Cutting feed rates are fast on plastics such as acrylic – we use 30mm per second feed, so as not to melt the acrylic.

2. Handle

The handle is built up from three parts – two sides and a middle spacer – so that when glued together, they will form a tight pocket

Fig. 7.18 The acrylic sheet.

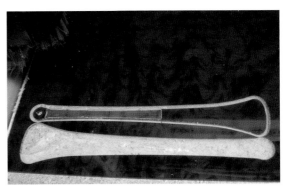

Fig. 7.19 Having just been cut out.

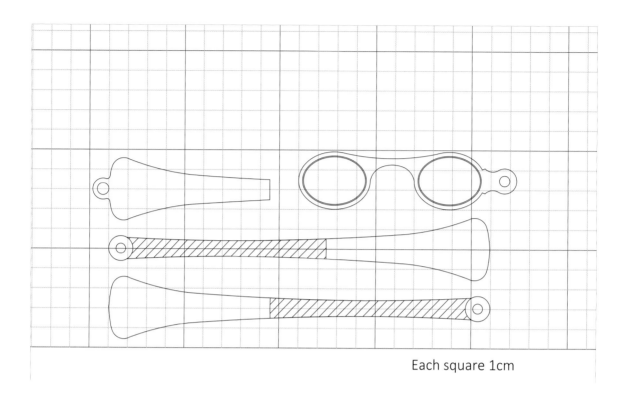

Each square 1cm

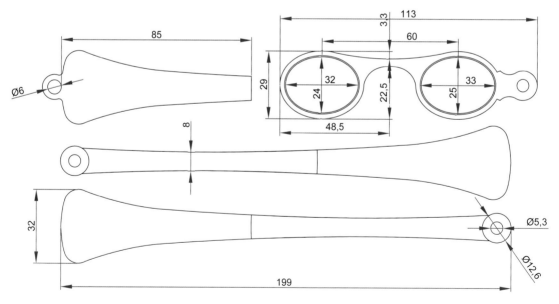

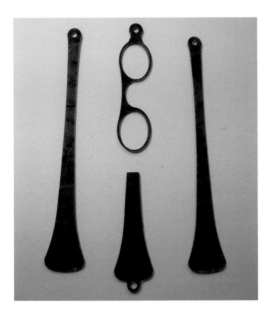

Fig. 7.20 All the components cut out.

Fig. 7.21 Showing the recess of the frame.

for the spectacles. To ease this problem, the area on the inner face of the sides where the spectacles will sit (the area shown hatched on the drawing) will be 'pocketed' to a depth of about 0.75mm giving clearance for the specs.

If the lorgnette was being made by any other method and pocketing was impractical, you should add an extra middle spacer layer of 1mm clear (to make a total of 4mm) to provide some clearance.

3. Lenses

The lenses are cut from 1mm clear acrylic to the profile of lens rebate, lifted from the spectacle drawing.

> **WARNING**
>
> Do not use real glass in prop eye-pieces. Original or professionally fitted spectacles should be fine with care.

4. Cutting

We have a small desk-top CNC, a Stepcraft, which cuts around A3 size. This has a 'spoil board' periodically fitted – a sheet of MDF or chipboard that acts as a work surface – and inevitably gets cut into, and damaged until requiring replacement. The tortoiseshell acrylic sheet is secured to the spoil sheet using TESA double-sided tape, which is strong enough to hold the sheet down without movement, while allowing the acrylic to be lifted off after cutting.

The actual cuts (using a ⅛ in single-flute cutter) take a maximum of ten minutes, if that.

The components are then lifted, and edges de-burred if necessary.

5. Assembly

The three (or four) parts of the handle are now placed one on top of the other, carefully lined up and making sure the clearance pockets are on the inside. The spectacle frames are temporarily fitted between the handle frames and secured with two-part nut-and-screw fixings ('Chicago screws') to ensure all parts are lined up. Once satisfied that all edges are flush, an appropriate solvent (E.M.A. Plastic Weld is one) is brushed round all the joints, allowing it to seep between the layers.

Once dry, the edges were lightly dressed with 600 grit wet-and-dry paper, followed by polishing with Duraglit/Brasso metal polish wadding.

6. Completion

The spectacles were completed by fitting the lenses. Each lens may need very light dressing with a fine file to ease the fit and epoxy glue then applied with a cocktail stick to the angle of the rebate. The lenses should then gently push into position, sitting into the depth of the frame.

Refit the spectacles with the screw fixing, ensuring that it is nipped up just tight enough to hold its position in the frame without drooping. If necessary, pack with a fine washer or file the fixing down to get the desired fit.

If making the spectacles without a rebate for the lens, then a good fit should be sufficient. Apply a thin bead or smear of epoxy all around the inside of the lens frame and then insert the lens into it. Again, any unfortunate mess on the lens may be cleaned up with a Brasso-soaked cotton bud.

> **TIP**
>
> If you get a smear of epoxy on the lens, use a cotton bud gently soaked in the Brasso wadding to polish the epoxy off.

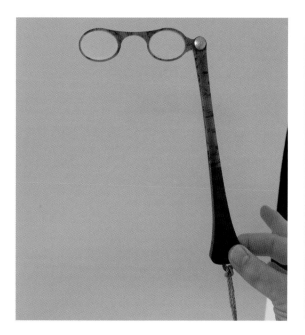

Fig. 7.22 The finished lorgnette.

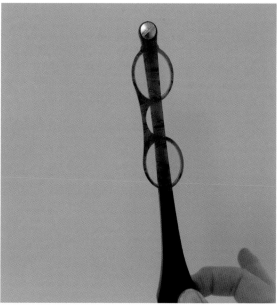

Fig. 7.23 Showing the folding mechanism.

FURTHER READING

JEWELLERY

- *The Visual History of Costume Accessories* by Valerie Cumming (1998). BT Batsford Ltd.
- *Designing & Making Jewellery* by Sarah Macrae (2001). The Crowood Press.
- *Jewels & Jewellery* by Clare Phillips (2000). V&A Publishing.
- *Art of the Islands: Celtic, Pictish, Anglo-Saxon and Viking Visual Culture, c. 450–1050* by Michelle P. Brown (2016). Bodleian Library (University of Oxford).

GLOVES

- *The Costume Accessories Series: Gloves* by Valerie Cummings (1982). BT Batsford Ltd.
- *Gloves: An Intimate History* by Anne Green (2021). Reaktion Books.

BAGS

- *Bags* by Clare Wilcox (2000). V&A Publications.
- *The Costume Accessories Series: Bags and Purses* by Vanda Foster (1982). BT Batsford Ltd.
- *The Visual History of Costume Accessories* by Valerie Cummings (1998). BT Batsford Ltd.

HATS

- *The Costume Accessories Series: Hats* by Fiona Clark (1982). BT Batsford Ltd.
- *Hats: A History of Fashion in Headwear* by Hilda Amphlett (1974). Dover Publications Inc.

CANES

- *Canes: From the Seventeenth to the Twentieth Century* by Jeffrey B. Snyder (1993). Schiffer Publishing.

TIARAS

- *Tiaras: Past and Present* by Geoffrey Munn (2002). V&A Publications.

SPECTACLES

- *Fashions in Eyeglasses: From the Fourteenth Century to the Present Day* by Richard Corson (1980). Peter Owen.

GLOSSARY

Ball Planisher	Either a shaped hammer or separate tool with a ball-shaped end, used to shape metal.
Ballpoint needles	Sewing needles with smooth ends used to sew jersey without cutting threads.
Blocking pins	Strong pins with large heads for ease of pushing used for blocking hats.
Borax	Cleaning product, also used as a flux in silver soldering and casting to ease the flow of the silver.
Breeches	Early men's trousers, either finishing just above or below the knee.
Cabochon stone	A stone milled with a flat back and domed front.
CAD program	Computer Aided Design program.
Chainmaille (Chain mail)	Linked metal rings, fabricated to protect, now can be 3D printed.
Chatelaine	A utility tool containing useful items, attached to a waist clip with chains or ribbons.
Clasp frame	A bag frame with a clip closure.
CNC Router	Computer Numerical Controlled shaping machine used to engrave and cut solid materials such as metal and wood.
Cool-paste	A clay used in jewellery soldering to keep delicate parts of the piece cool while heating.
Diode lasers	A semiconductor laser, similar to an LED, allowing a very fine cutting light.
Electroplating	The process of coating a surface with metal using electricity.
FDM	Fused Deposition Modelling – filament printing.
Flux	Liquid or paste used in soldering and silver-soldering.
Fourchettes	The parts of gloves giving the depth of the fingers.
French wire or gimp	Fine metal and fabric sprung cord for use when attaching fastenings.
Gas lasers	These convert electricity to light energy and produce an infrared cutting light.
Hat Block	An internal hat shape made in wood, metal or high-density polystyrene used to mould or shape hats.
Jeweller's glue	A strong, fast-drying glue.
Jeweller's peg	A small, shaped platform, usually in wood clamped to a worktable and used during jewellery making.
Lace straw ribbon	Straw braided into lace.
MDF	Medium Density Fibreboard, used in carpentry projects.
Needle files	Small metal or wood files, used in small projects.
Nickel silver	An alloy of copper, nickel and zinc that gives the appearance of silver.
Penannular	An early form of brooch, made with an open ring and pin.
Petersham	A tape made with thicker weft threads, giving a stiff support for hats and waistbands.

Pewter	A soft metal made from an alloy of tin, copper and lead.
Pickle	A solution, either acid or alkali, used to clean metal pieces of fire/heat damage, the most common nowadays is sodium bisulphate, though vinegar or lemon juice can also be used.
Piercing saw	A framed saw with fine blades, so called because it can be placed through a drilled hole and used to cut out an inner edge of a shape.
PLA filament	Polylactic acid, a filament that melts with heat and is used in 3D printing.
Plywood	Sheet wood made from alternating grained layers of wood.
Pop rivets	Aluminium rivets with central core that is used to shape the rivet with a drawing tool.
Potassium Permanganate	An equine disinfectant that is an effective way of dyeing fabric various shades of brown.
Resin printers	Photo-solidification that creates polymers during 3D printing.
Ring mandrel	A smooth rod of tapered steel used to shape and size rings in jewellery making.
Ring sizer	A tapered rod with ring sizes marked used to test the size of a ring.
Silicone rubber	A rubber-like material, consisting of silicon (plastic) with carbon, hydrogen and oxygen.
Silver solder	A metal with a high content of silver but a lower melting point, used to join metal.
Silver-solder paste	Silver solder made into a paste including flux making it easier to silver solder.
Skiver	A bladed tool for shaving down the edges of leather (also used to thin areas of leather).
Slip stitch	A hemming stitch created by taking the thread through the edge of one side and taking a very small amount of fabric from the other.
Smooth-faced pliers	Jewellers use pliers without ridges on the grip – normal pliers may have these filed off so as not to mark the soft metal.
Soft solder	A lead-based solder, softer than silver solder, used for joining metal.
Solvent	A liquid in which another dissolves or dilutes, used in this case to help melting or cleaning.
Straw ribbon	Lengths of straw, braided into ribbons.
Toile	A mock-up of a garment in a cheap fabric in order to try out the pattern for size and style before using the final fabric.
Tortoiseshell	Real tortoiseshell was taken from the hawkbill Sea turtle and is mimicked in acrylic and other plastics. Also, many things resembling the pattern are named as such.
Transfer pencil	A pencil used to transfer patterns from paper to material.
Treble stitch	In crochet, this is a stitch where the thread is wrapped round the crochet hook 3 times, the hook taken through the pattern and brought through each resulting loop, one at a time.
Vegetable tan leather	Leather tanned with a natural tannin, taken from plants such as Oak and Spruce bark.
Warp	The threads on a weaving loom running the length of the fabric, also used to describe the same direction on non-woven fabrics.
Weft	The threads on a weaving loom running across the fabric, also used to describe the same direction on non-woven fabrics.

INDEX